English for Life

Beginner

Workbook with key

Tom Hutchinson

OXFORD

1 Introducing yourself Numbers

1 Complete the conversation.

Mike [1]H*e l l o*. [2]M___ name's Mike.

Irena [3]P______________ to [4]m_______ you, Mike. [5]I'___ Irena Larsen.

Mike [6]N_______ to meet [7]y_____ too, Irena.

Irena What's [8]y_______ surname?

Mike My [9]s_______________ is Hall.

2 Make sentences. Use short forms.

1 I am Irena.

I'm Irena.

2 What is your name?

____

3 My name is Mike.

____

4 I am Pedro.

____

5 My surname is Hall.

____

3 Complete the crossword. Use numbers 0–10.

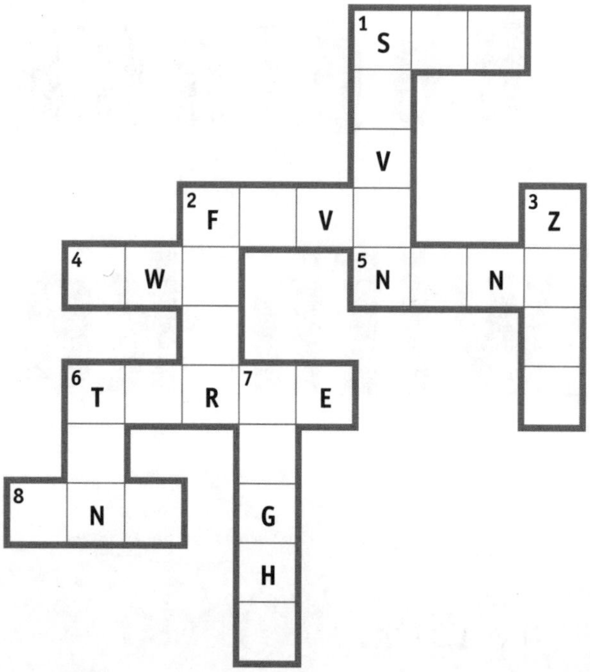

4 Write the phone numbers.

1 My phone number is oh, one, seven, two, six – double two, five, eight double nine; and my mobile number is oh, double seven, nine, five – eight, nine, two, four, double three.

Home *01726 225899*

Mobile ______________________________

2 My home number is oh two oh – six, double one – seven, oh, nine, five; and my mobile is oh, seven, nine, two, oh – five, double six, double four, eight.

Home ______________________________

Mobile ______________________________

5 Answer the questions.

1 What's your first name?

My first name's ______________________________

2 What's your surname?

____

3 What's your phone number?

It's oh, ... ______________________________

4 What's your mobile number?

____

6 Complete the sentences about yourself.

Hi! My name's ______________________________,

and my surname's ______________________________.

My home phone number is ______________________________,

and my mobile number is ______________________________.

✓ **Now ...** ***practise and learn.***

2 *a / an* + singular nouns *this* and *that*

1 Complete the crossword.

Across

Down

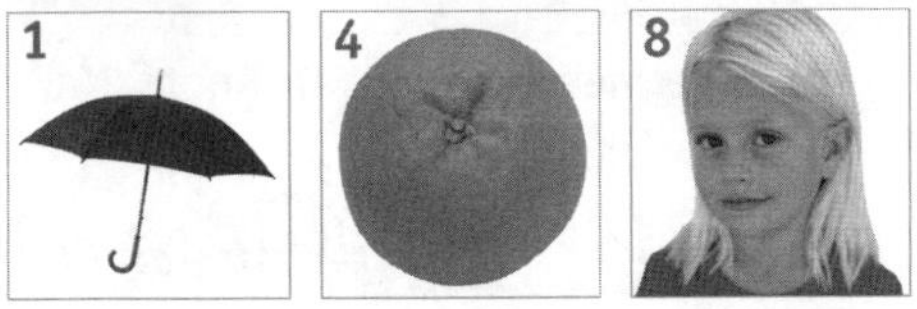

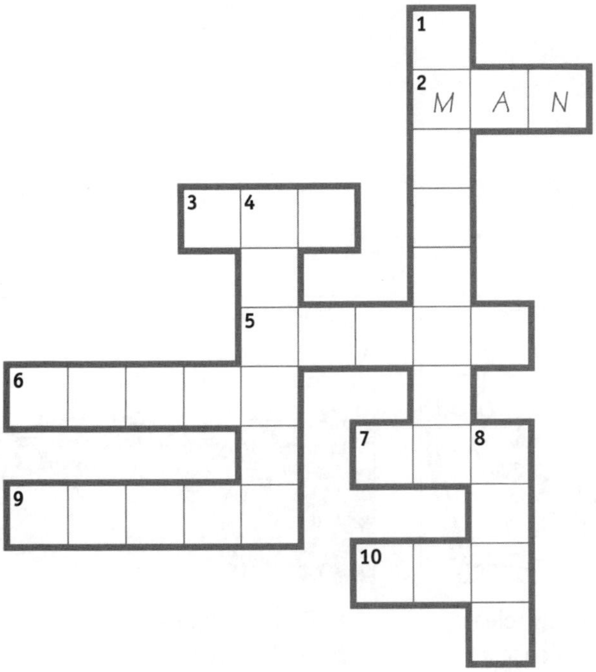

2 Complete the table. Use the words in the box.

~~chair~~ ~~apple~~ book pencil eraser
table umbrella orange pen computer

a	*an + a / e / i / o / u*
a chair	*an apple*
________	________
________	________
________	________
________	
________	

3 Complete the sentences. Use *this* or *that*.

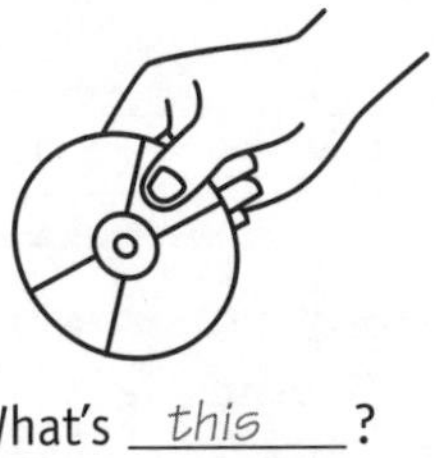

1 What's *this*?

2 What's ________?

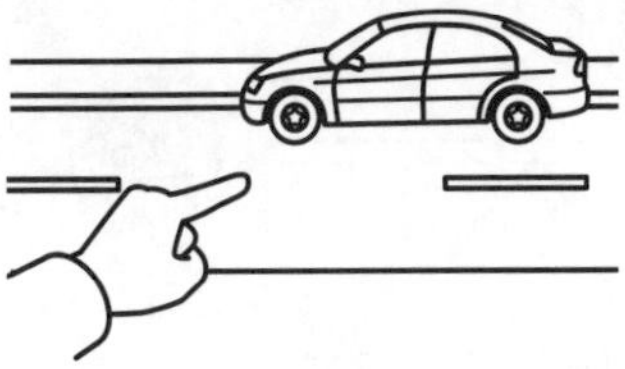

3 ________'s my car.

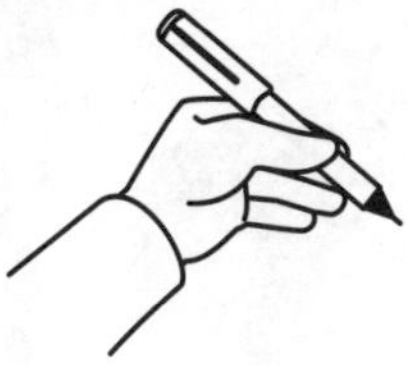

4 ________ is my pen.

5 ________ is my umbrella.

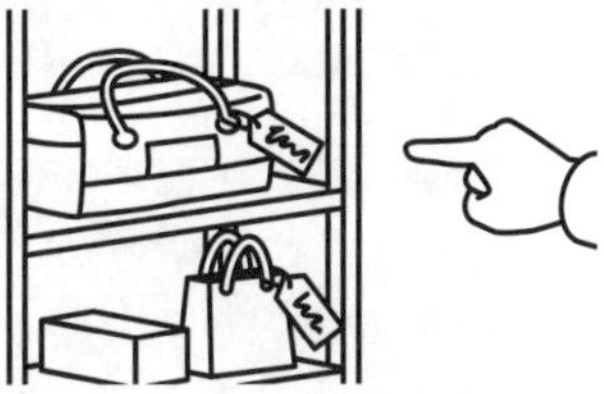

6 ________'s my bag.

4 Complete the conversations. Use the words in the box.

English means ~~does~~ say mean do

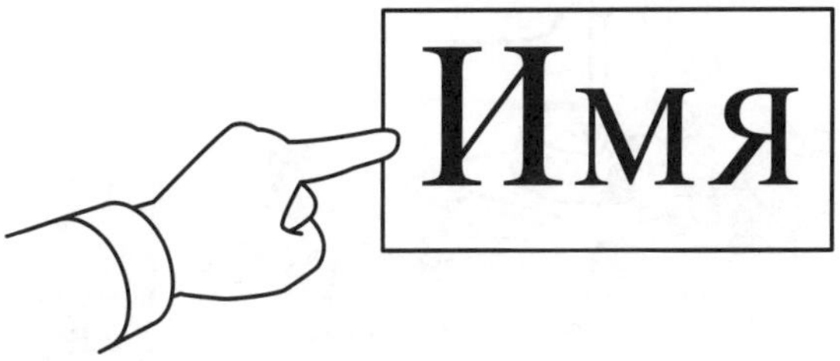

1 **A** What [1] *does* this [2]________?

B It [3]________ 'name'.

2 **A** How [1]________ you say 'Bienvenido' in [2]________?

B You [3]________ 'Welcome'.

3 Classroom language Instructions

1 Label the things in the picture.

2 Choose the correct instructions.

1 a Don't listen to this.
  b Listen to this. ✓

2 a Don't open the window, please.
  b Open the window, please.

3 a Don't look at that car!
  b Look at that car!

4 a Don't close the door, please.
  b Close the door, please.

5 a Don't write your name here.
  b Write your name here, please.

6 a Read this, please.
  b Don't read this, please.

3 Complete the conversations.

1
A What does 'occupation' mean?
B I'm sorry. I d_____'t k_____.

2
A What's your first name?
B I'm sorry, c___n you r___p______t, that, please?
A Yes. What's your first name?
B Oh, my name's Ivan.

3
A The meeting's in Room 10.
B I'm s_______y. I don't u___d____s_______d.
A The meeting – it's in Room 10.
B Oh, OK. Thanks!

✓ **Now ...** ***practise and learn.***

4 The alphabet and spelling
Review: lessons 1–4

1 Write the missing letters and find the hidden word.

4__ 5__ C D 6__ F G 3__

I J K 1 L M N O 2__ Q

R S 7__ U V W X Y Z

The hidden word is

A 1 L 2__ 3__ 4__ 5__ 6__ 7__ .

2 Choose the correct words.

Jordan What's 1~~you~~ / <u>your</u> last 2*name / surname*, Cindy?
Cindy 3*My name's / I'm* Gaskell.
Jordan 4*How / What* do you 5*say / spell* that?
Cindy It's G-A-S-K, E 6*double / repeat* L.
Jordan 7*Please / Thank you*.

3 Complete the conversation. Use the words in the box.

sorry	meet	~~this~~	my	nice	name

Alan John, 1 *this* is my friend, Karen.
John Nice to 2________ you, Karen.
Karen 3________ to meet you, too. I'm 4________. What's your 5________ again?
John 6________ name's John. John Dunn.

4 Write the conversation in the correct order.

Here you are.
Tea, please.
Thanks, Ivana.
~~Tea or coffee, Marco?~~

Ivana *Tea or coffee, Marco?*
Marco ________________
Ivana ________________
Marco ________________

Lessons 1–4

Choose the correct words and rewrite the sentences.

1 *I / My* name's Sasha. ________________
2 Nice *to / two* meet you. ________________
3 What *does / is* 'surname' mean? ________________
4 *No / Don't* open the door. ________________
5 What's *you / your* first name? ________________
6 This *is / it* my friend, Carlo. ________________
7 That's *a / an* umbrella. ________________
8 *I / I'm* sorry. I don't understand. ________________

✓ **Now ...** ***review your progress.***

5 Family members
Possessive 's

1a Complete the family words.

	M	O	T	1 H	E	R				
		D	A	2	G	H	T	E	R	
		S	I	3	T	E	R			
				4	R	O	T	H	E	R
			F	5	T	H	E	R		
P	A	R	E	6	T	S				
C	H	I	L	7	R	E	N			

b Find the hidden word.

The hidden word is 1 H 2___ 3___ 4___ 5___ 6___ 7___.

2 Complete the sentences.

1

2

3

4

3 Complete the sentences.

1 This is Daniel's car.

2 This is __________ __________ book.

3 This is __________ and __________ phone number.

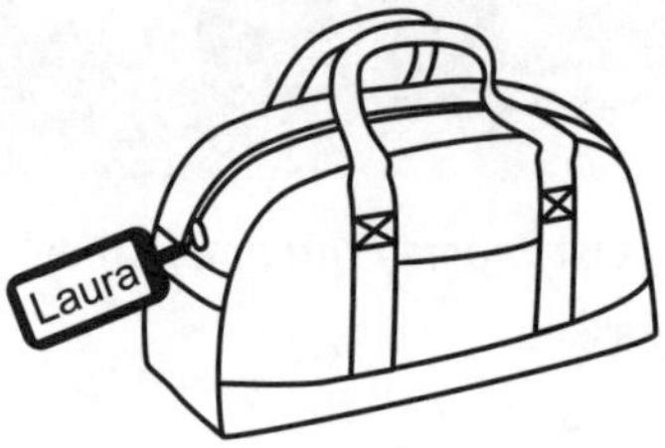

4 This is __________ bag.

4 Rewrite the sentences. Use full forms.

1 That's Helen's husband.
That is Helen's husband.

2 He's Maria's friend.
____

3 She's Jim's wife.
____

4 What's Miguel's number?
____

5 Sarah's here.
____

6 What's Peter's surname?
____

6 Possessive adjectives

1 Complete the conversations. Use *his* or *her*.

1 **A** This is Tim's office. That's __his__ desk over there.

B What's ________ name again?

A Tim. He's my boss.

2 **A** What's ________ name?

B She's Antonia.

A And what's ________ name?

B He's Ben. He's ________ boyfriend.

3 **A** This is my sister. ________ name's Carla. And this is ________ husband. ________ name's Harry.

B Hello Carla, hello Harry.

2 Complete the conversations. Use the cues.

1 my / your

A Hello. __My__ name's Roman. What's ________ name?

B ________ name's Tania.

2 his / her

A What's ________ name?

B ________ name's Maria. And that's ________ husband.

A What's ________ name?

B ________ name's José.

3 my / her / his / your

A Is this photo ________ son with ________ wife?

B No, it isn't. That's ________ daughter with ________ husband!

4 its / my / our

A This photo is ________ husband Claudio, and that's ________ house. ________ name is 'Monticello'.

3 Complete the sentences. Use the words in the box.

her their (x2) its his (x2) ~~our~~

This is a photo of 1 __our__ holiday hotel in Mexico. 2 ________ name is Hotel Azul. This is the hotel manager. 3 ________ name's Juan Carlos. This is 4 ________ wife. 5 ________ name's Carmen and these are 6 ________ children, Roberto and Ana. 7 ________ daughter Juanita isn't in the picture. She's eighteen, and she's a singer. It's a great hotel.

Describing family
Pronunciation: The phonemic alphabet

1 Read the texts. Write the names.

1

This is my brother, Yves, with his wife and children. His wife's name is Sonia. His daughter's name is Véronique and his son's name is Philippe. The dog's name is Bruno.

a ____________________

b ____________________

c ____________________

d ____________________

e ____________________

2 *These are my parents. My dad's name is Jacek and my mum's name is Ewa. That's my sister, Jola, and my brother. His name's Marek. He's a student.*

a ____________________

b ____________________

c ____________________

d ____________________

3 Write about your family.

My father's name is …

____

____

____

____

____

____

____

4 Pronunciation Complete the table. Use the words in the box.

~~nine~~	are	friend	wife
he	read	ten	car

/aɪ/	five, *nine*, write, ________
/ɑː/	father, ________, class, ________
/iː/	please, ________, three, ________
/e/	yes, ________, spell, ________

2 Choose the correct words.

1 These are my *parents* / ~~*fathers*~~.

2 This is my *mum* / *dad*. *His* / *Her* name's Shekhar.

=

3 This is my *mum* / *dad*. *His* / *Her* name's Sarla.

4 This is my *wife* / *husband*. *His* / *Her* name's Kalpana.

=

5 This is me. *My* / *Your* name's Vijay.

6 This is my *sister* / *brother*. *His* / *Her* name's Amul.

7 These are our *sons* / *children*. *Their* / *Our* names are Pradeep and Komal.

8 Saying hello and goodbye
Review: lessons 5–8

1 Delete the incorrect expressions.

1 Hello. / Goodbye. / Good morning. / See you.

2 Good evening. / Good night. / Goodbye. / Hi.

2 Number the conversation in the correct order.

a ___ OK. See you later.

b _1_ Hello, Mark.

c ___ I'm fine, thanks. And you?

d ___ Hi, Kathy. How are you?

e ___ Yes, bye.

f _4_ Fine.

✓ **Now ...** ***practise and learn.***

3 Choose the correct expressions.

1 a Good morning, Ms Johar.
  b Good morning, Mr Johar. ✓

2 a Good evening, Miss Kovács.
  b Good evening, Miss Andrea Kovács.

3 a That's Miss Taylor and her husband.
  b That's Mrs Taylor and her husband.

4 a Good evening, Ms Bates.
  b Hi, Claire.

Lessons 5–8

Make conversations. Match the expressions with the responses.

1 Hello. What's your name? ___
2 Hi. I'm Gina Lear. ___
3 What's this? ___
4 Good morning. ___
5 What's your phone number? ___
6 How do you spell your first name? ___
7 Who's that? ___
8 What's your father's name? ___

a Good morning.
b It's *K-I-R, S-T-Y*. Kirsty.
c His name's Pierre.
d Pleased to meet you, Gina.
e My name's Bill May.
f That's my boss.
g It's 07534 887963.
h It's my English book.

✓ **Now ...** ***review your progress.***

9 Countries
Pronunciation: Stress

1a Complete the names of the countries.
b Label two more countries on the map.

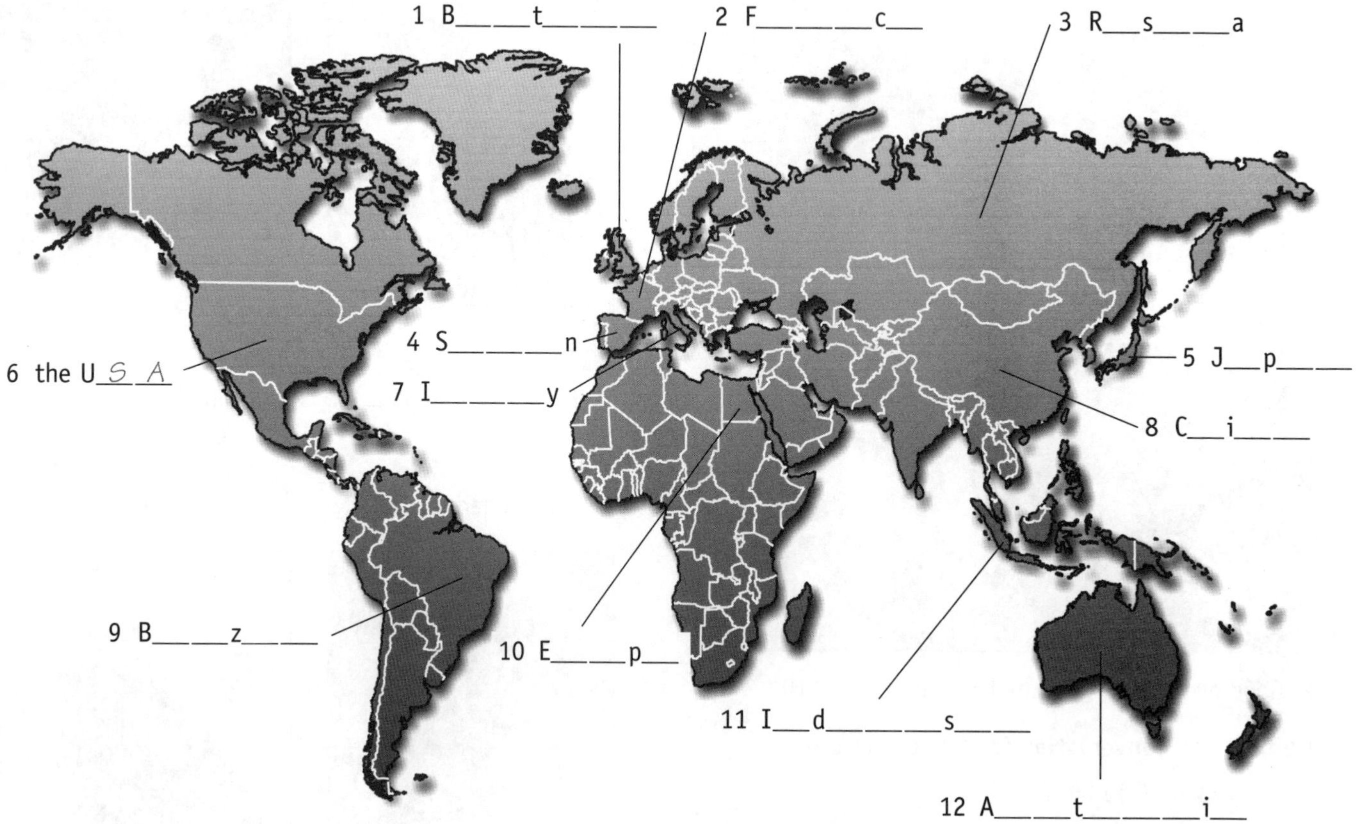

2 Rewrite the sentences with correct capital letters.

1 cairo is the capital of egypt.
Cairo is the capital of Egypt.

2 sydney is in australia.
____

3 my favourite country is china.
____

4 my favourite city is new york.
____

5 is antonio from spain?
____

6 my home is in poland.
____

7 rome is the capital of italy.
____

8 he's from argentina.
____

3 Complete the sentences.

1 I'm from ________________. (*your country*)
2 My home is in ________________. (*your city*)
3 ________________ is the capital of my country.
4 My favourite country is ________________.
5 My favourite city is ________________.

✓ Now ... *practise and learn.*

4 Mark the syllable with the stress.

1 Hungary	6 Japan
2 Korea	7 Italy
3 Australia	8 America
4 Brazil	9 Indonesia
5 Russia	10 Britain

10 *to be*: positive and negative
Saying where people are from

1 Put the words in the correct order to make sentences. Punctuate your sentences with capital letters and full stops.

1 am from i france

I am from France.

2 student a is john

3 in moscow russia is

4 from we china are

5 are my from friends italy

6 she my is daughter

7 husband my is usa the from

8 am teacher a i

2 Rewrite the sentences. Use full forms.

1 We're students.

We are students.

2 I'm from New York.

3 They're his friends.

4 She's from Greece.

5 Dan's my husband.

6 I'm her sister.

7 Manchester's in the UK.

8 You're in Room 9.

3 Make the sentences negative.

1 She's the Managing Director.

She isn't the Managing Director.

2 I'm at my desk.

3 This is my mobile.

4 They're brother and sister.

5 We're from Shanghai.

6 Lukas is in his office.

7 I'm married.

8 You're in this photo.

9 My boss is here.

10 Our children are here.

4 Complete the sentences about your life.

1 I'm ____________.

2 I'm not ____________.

3 My teacher's ____________.

4 My teacher isn't ____________.

5 My parents are ____________.

6 My parents aren't ____________.

7 My friends are ____________.

8 They aren't ____________.

✓ **Now ...** ***practise and learn.***

11 *he's* and *his*
Reading and writing: personal information

1a Make sentences. Use the cues.

1 I / student
I'm a student.

2 She / not / teacher
______

3 He / doctor
______

4 My sister / engineer
______

5 You / student
______

6 I / computer engineer
______

b Add more information to your sentences in exercise 1a. Use the cues with *and*.

1 Russia
I'm a student and I'm from Russia.

2 not / China
______

3 South Africa
______

4 the Czech Republic
______

5 Italy
______

6 Brazil
______

2 Complete the sentences. Use *he's* or *his*.

1 *He's* a doctor.

2 *His* brother is at university.

3 ______ from Argentina.

4 What's ______ name?

5 **A** Where's Pedro?

B ______ over there.

6 This is my friend, Tom. ______ in this photo with ______ parents.

3a Read the text. Complete the table. Use the words in the box.

Haru's boyfriend	Daisuke	Jane's husband	Australia
an English teacher	a doctor	an engineer	~~Japan~~

My name's Haru and I'm from Osaka in Japan. I'm an English teacher. In this picture I'm at a party with my boyfriend. His name's Daisuke. He's a student at Tokyo University. He isn't from Japan. He's from San Francisco in the USA. We're with my friend, Jane, and her husband. Jane's a doctor. Her husband's name is Dieter. He's an engineer. Jane and Dieter aren't from Japan. Jane's from Australia and Dieter's from Germany.

Name	From	Job	Relationship
Haru	1 *Japan*	2 ______	Daisuke's girlfriend
3 ______	the USA	a student	4 ______
Jane	5 ______	6 ______	Dieter's wife
Dieter	Germany	7 ______	8 ______

b Write two sentences about each person. Use the table. Connect the information with *and*.

1 Haru *'s from Japan* and *she's an English teacher.*
She's Daisuke's girlfriend.

2 Daisuke ______ and ______
______

3 Jane ______ and ______
______

4 Dieter ______ and ______
______

4 Now write two sentences about yourself and a person in your family, or a friend.

1 I'm ______ (*country*),
and I'm a / an ______ (*job*).
I'm ______ (*relationship*).

2 ______
and ______.
______.

12 Saying sorry
Review: lessons 9–12

1a Match the parts of the expressions.

1 I'm very _d_ a fine.
2 I'm ___ b OK?
3 It's all ___ c right.
4 Are you ___ d sorry.

b Complete the conversation. Use the expressions in exercise 1a to help you.

A I'm [1] _very_ _sorry_. Are [2]________ ________?
B Yes. It's [3]________ ________. I'm [4]________, thank you.

2 Put the words in the correct order. Write the expressions in the bubbles.

hand my   sorry very I'm   right all it's

you OK are   thank fine I'm you

Lessons 9–12

Correct the sentences.

1 I'm from russia.
____

2 She's doctor.
____

3 His in the office.
____

4 Am not married.
____

5 He's from USA.
____

6 They're from the France.
____

7 This is Johns phone.
____

8 We isn't in Room 10.
____

9 This is book.
____

10 You're desk's over there.
____

✓ **Now ...** ***review your progress.***

13 Numbers 11–100

1 Find the numbers in the word snake.

53 42 ~~30~~ 81 98 60 ~~65~~ 19 13 50 77 24

thirtysixty-fivefiftynineteenninety-eightfifty-threetwenty-foureighty-onesixtythirteenseventy-sevenforty-two

2a Complete the table.

2 *two*	12 twelve	20 ______
3 three	13 ______	30 thirty
4 ______	14 fourteen	40 ______
5 five	15 ______	50 fifty
6 ______	16 sixteen	60 ______
7 seven	17 ______	70 seventy
8 ______	18 eighteen	80 ______
9 nine	19 ______	90 ninety

b **Pronunciation** **Find these numbers in the table above, and mark the stress.**

~~13~~ ~~30~~ 14 40 15 50 16 60 17 70 18 80 19 90

thirteen thirty

3 Correct the mistakes.

1 **21** twentyone *twenty-one*
2 **52** fivety-two ______
3 **86** eighteen-six ______
4 **12** twelfe ______
5 **11** elleven ______
6 **91** ninety-two ______
7 **45** fourty-five ______
8 **14** forteen ______
9 **100** an hundred ______
10 **68** sixty eight ______
11 **33** thirteen-three ______
12 **79** sixty-nineteen ______

4 Match the sentences with the pictures.

1 My bus is number **fifty-three.** *e*
2 My English lesson is in room number **eighty-seven.** __
3 I'm size **thirty-eight.** __
4 I'm **thirty.** __
5 My friend is **twenty-five.** __
6 Our home is number **nineteen.** __

a

b

c

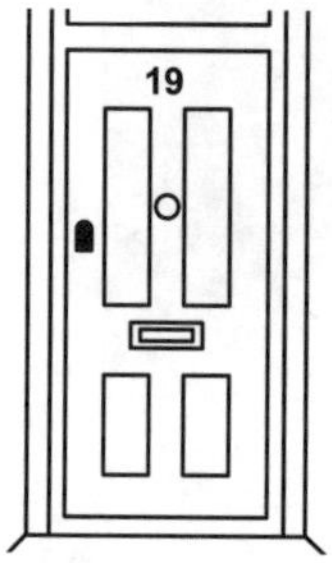

d

e

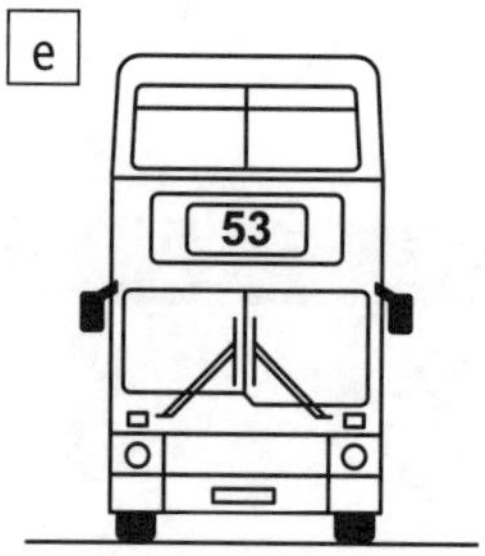

f

5 Change the bold words in exercise 4 to make the sentences true for you.

1 My bus is ______
2 ______
3 ______
4 ______
5 ______
6 ______

✓ **Now ...** *practise and learn.*

14 *to be*: questions and short answers
Writing: a short paragraph about yourself

1 Make questions.

1 You're Lucy Scott.
Are you Lucy Scott?

2 He's on holiday.
______ on holiday?

3 That is ABC Computer Services.
______ ABC Computer Services?

4 We're in Room 9.
______ in Room 9?

5 They're from Indonesia.
______ from Indonesia?

6 You're a doctor.
______ a doctor?

2 Choose the correct short answers.

1 Is Mr James an engineer?
Yes, he is. / ~~No, it isn't.~~

2 Are you from Slovenia?
No, we're aren't. / Yes, you are.

3 Are Sam and Ella married?
Yes, we are. / No, they aren't.

4 Is this your office?
No, it isn't. / Yes, I am.

5 Are you a doctor?
Yes, I am. / No, we aren't.

3 Complete the short answers.

1 Is this your mobile?
No, it *isn't*.

2 Is Lucy married?
No, she ______.

3 Are you Sergei Ivanov?
Yes, I ______.

4 Is the meeting in your office?
Yes, it ______.

5 Are we in Mr Marsh's English class?
No, we ______.

6 Are Mr Leclerc and Mrs Casson from France?
Yes, they ______.

4 Put the words in the correct order to make questions. Use the correct punctuation.

1 is how old Juan ?
How old is Juan?

2 they are where from ?
______

3 where your office is ?
______

4 your children how old are ?
______

5 what her name is ?
______

6 is his phone number what ?
______

5 Answer the questions.

1 What's your name?
My name's ______.

2 Where are you from?
I'm ______.

3 How old are you?
I'm ______.

4 Are you a student?
______.

5 Are you married?
______.

6 What is your teacher's name?
It's ______.

6 Write a paragraph about yourself.

My name's ______ and I'm from ______. I'm ______ years old and I'm a / an ______ (*job*). I'm ______ (*single / married / divorced*). My ______ (*wife's / husband's / teacher's*) name is ______.

✓ **Now ...** *practise and learn.*

15 Asking for and giving personal information
Writing: completing a form

1 Choose the correct words.

a How *old* / ~~*age*~~ are you?
b What's your *one* / *first* name?
c Where are you *of* / *from*?
d What's *you* / *your* phone number?
e *Is* / *Are* you married?
f *Where's* / *What's* your surname?

2 Complete the conversation. Write the questions from exercise 1 in the correct places.

Agent 1 *What's your surname?*
Anita It's Moretti.
Agent 2 ______________________
Anita Anita. That's A-N-I-T-A.
Agent Thank you. 3 ______________________
Anita I'm from Italy.
Agent 4 ______________________, Ms Moretti?
Anita I'm 24 years old.
Agent 5 ______________________
Anita No, I'm not. I'm single.
Agent OK. 6 ______________________
Anita It's 0209, 736, 5 double 2.
Agent Thank you.

3 Match the questions in exercise 1 with the correct parts of the personal information form.

Please complete your personal details.

Question	Information	Anita	You
f	Surname	*Moretti*	______
______	First name	______	______
______	Country	______	______
______	Age	______	______
______	Marital status	______	______
______	Tel. No.	______	______

4a Read the conversation in exercise 2 again. Complete the form in exercise 3 for Anita.

b Now complete the form for yourself.

5 Write your own conversation with the agent. Use the form in exercise 3 to help you.

Agent 1 ____________ ____________ surname?
You It's 2 ____________.
Agent What's 3 ____________ first ____________?
You It's 4 ____________.
Agent Thank you. And where 5 ____________ ____________ ____________?
You I'm from 6 ____________.
Agent How old 7 ____________ ____________, please?
You I'm 8 ____________ years old.
Agent 9 ____________ ____________ married?
You 10 ____________, I ____________.
Agent OK. And what's your 11 ____________ ____________, please?
You It's 12 ____________.
Agent Thank you very much.

✓ **Now ...** ***practise and learn.***

16 Telling the time
Review: lessons 13–16

1 Match the times with the watches.

1 It's twelve oh two. _c_
2 It's ten ten. __
3 It's three fifteen. __
4 It's twenty-one twenty-five. __
5 It's three fifty. __
6 It's eight thirty. __

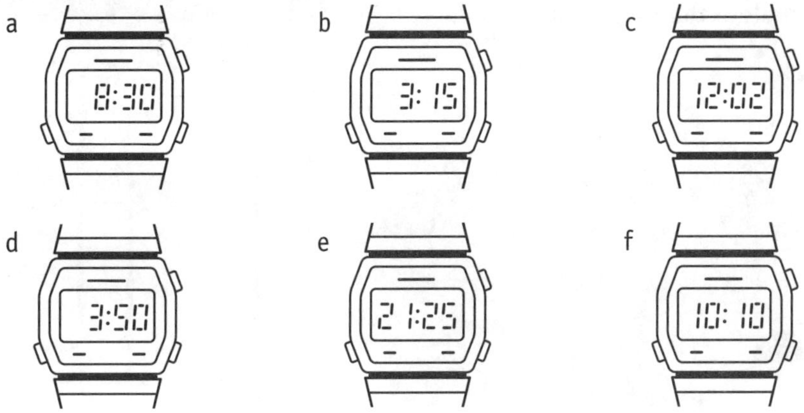

2 Write the times.

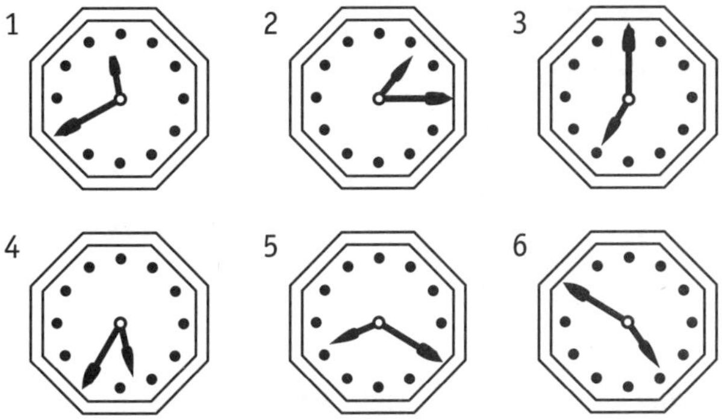

1 _It's twenty to twelve._
2 ______
3 ______
4 ______
5 ______
6 ______

3 Complete the sentences. Write information about your country.

Opening times in ______

Shops	Shops are open from ______ to ______.
Supermarkets	Supermarkets are open from ______ to ______.
Banks	Banks are open from ______ to ______.
Cafés and bars	Cafés and bars are open from ______ to ______.
Offices	Normal office hours are from ______ to ______.

Lessons 13–16

Match the questions with the answers.

1 Is this your mobile? __
2 How old are you? __
3 What's the time? __
4 Where are you from? __
5 Is Lola a teacher? __
6 What number is your house? __
7 What's your surname? __
8 Are you married? __

a No, I'm not.
b It's number fifty-one.
c Yes, she is.
d I'm twenty-two.
e It's seven o'clock.
f No, it isn't.
g We're from Brazil.
h It's Casson.

✓ **Now …** ***review your progress.***

17 Things people carry
Pronunciation: syllables

1 Complete the picture crossword.

Across ➧

Down ⬇

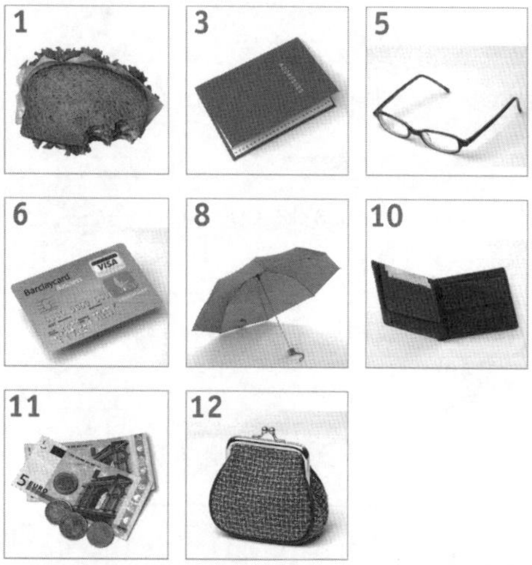

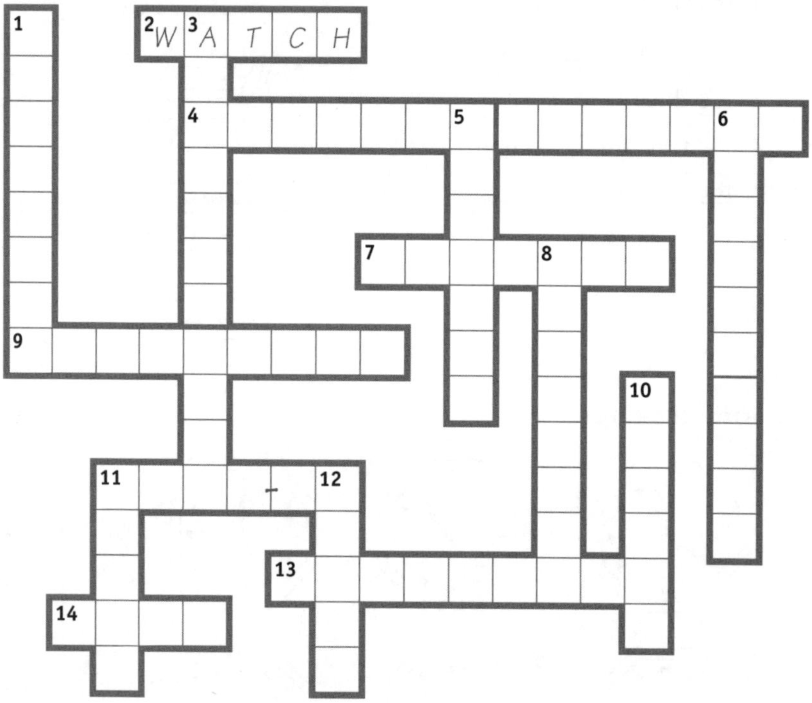

2 Complete the table.

	Singular	Plural
1	*a wallet*	wallets
2	a dog	*dogs*
3	______	children
4	______	women
5	______	watches
6	a man	______
7	______	hairbrushes
8	a key	______
9	______	sandwiches
10	______	people

3 What's in your bag, briefcase or pockets?

In my pocket – three keys, a wallet …

____

In my bag – an English book, a pencil …

____

____

4a Pronunciation How many syllables? Write the number in the brackets.

b Tick (✓) the words with an extra syllable in the plural.

	Singular (syllables)	Plural (syllables)	Extra syllable?
1	pencil (2)	pencils (*2*)	
2	watch (1)	watches (*2*)	✓
3	briefcase (2)	briefcases (__)	
4	umbrella (3)	umbrellas (__)	
5	apple (2)	apples (__)	
6	purse (1)	purses (__)	
7	tissue (2)	tissues (__)	
8	licence (2)	licences (__)	
9	orange (2)	oranges (__)	
10	key (1)	keys (__)	

18 Saying where things are *a/an* and *the*

1 Match the sentences with the correct cars.

a

b

c

d

e

f

1 Paula is behind her car. _d_
2 Gustav is under his car. ___
3 Ella's cat is on her car. ___
4 Omar's car is next to the shop. ___
5 Dave is in front of his car. ___
6 Nina is in her car. ___

2 Complete the sentences.

1 The newspaper is _next to_ the clock.
2 The books are ______________ the box.
3 The umbrella is ______________ the box.
4 The bag is ______________ the chair.
5 The clock is ______________ the chair.
6 The box is ______________ the chair.

3 Complete the phrases and sentences. Use *a / an* or *the*.

1 _an_ apple _a_ book
The apple is on _the_ book.

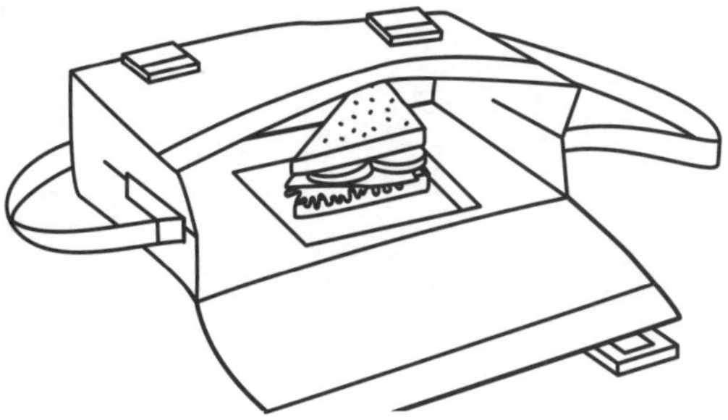

2 _____ sandwich _____ bag
_____ sandwich is in _____ bag.

3 _____ umbrella _____ chair
_____ umbrella is under _____ chair.

4 _____ key _____ wallet
_____ key is in _____ wallet.

19 Prices
Going shopping

1 Match the labels with the prices.

a
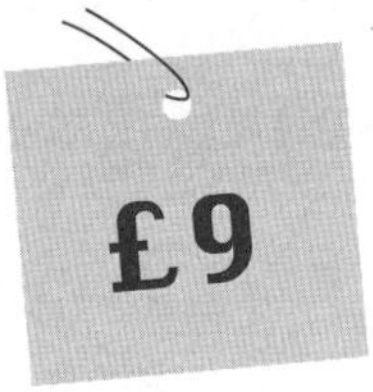

b
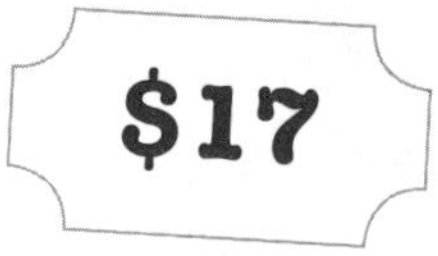

c

d

e
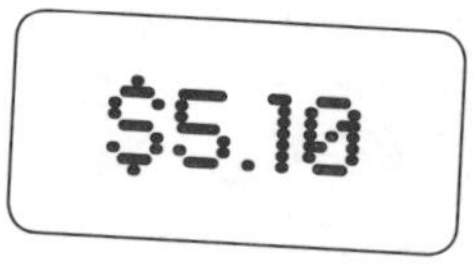

f
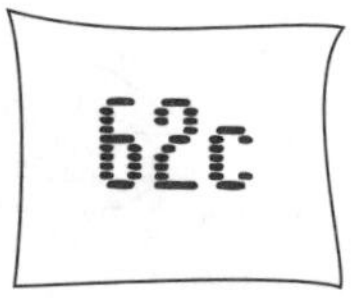

g
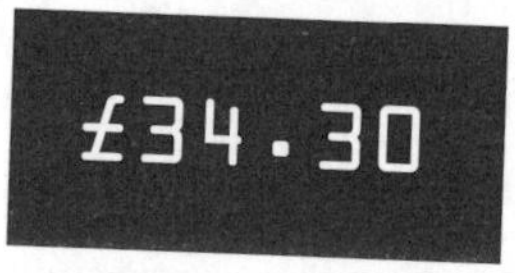

h

1 Seventeen dollars _b_
2 Ninety-nine pence __
3 Thirty-four pounds thirty __
4 Sixty-two cents __
5 Four euros __
6 Twenty euros seventy cents __
7 Five dollars ten cents __
8 Nine pounds __

2 Complete the sentences. Choose the correct words.

1 How much is *this* / ~~*these*~~ briefcase?
2 How much are *that* / *those* hairbrushes?
3 Can I have *these* / *that* purse, please?
4 How much are *this* / *those* pens?
5 Can I have *that* / *these* bag please?
6 How much are *those* / *this* sunglasses?

3a Complete the conversation. Use the questions in the box.

Can I have that one, please?	~~Can I help you?~~
How much are those wallets?	Anything else?

Assistant [1] *Can I help you?*
Customer Yes. [2] ____________
Assistant They're €65 each.
Customer [3] ____________
Assistant Certainly. [4] ____________
Customer No, thank you.

b Write a new conversation. Use the cues.
these bags / £28 / this one

Assistant Can I [1] ____________?
Customer Yes. How [2] ____________ ____________?
Assistant They're [3] ____________.
Customer Can I [4] ____________, please?
Assistant [5] ____________. [6] ____________ else?
Customer No, [7] ____________.

4 Complete the signs.

1 P _u_ _s_ H

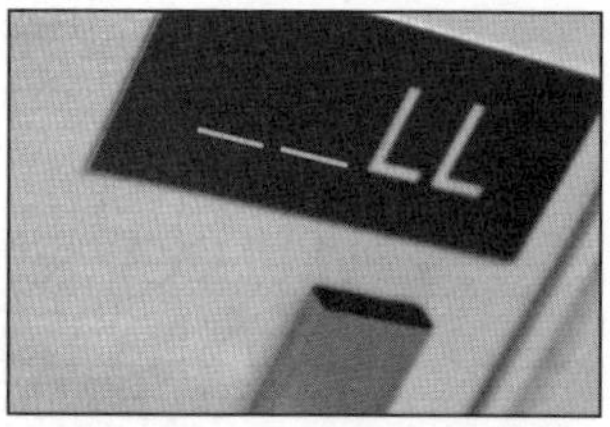

2 ___ ___ L L

3 O P ___ ___

4 C L ___ ___ ___ D

5 E X ___ ___

6 T o i ___ ___ t

20 Inviting someone for a drink
Review: lessons 17–20

1 Match the parts of the sentences about Episode 3 of the story.

1 The meeting is with _f_
2 The meeting is in __
3 The meeting is at __
4 The photographs are at __
5 Daniel invites Lucy to __
6 Lucy goes to the pub for __

a the pub.
b a few minutes.
c Cambridge.
d half past ten tomorrow.
e The Photo Shop.
f Mr Linksy from Top Films.

2 Number the conversation in the correct order.

a __ **Lucy** Oh, hi, Daniel. I'd love to, but I can't.
b _1_ **Daniel** Hey, Lucy. We're off to the pub. Are you coming?
c __ **Lucy** Oh, OK, but only for a few minutes.
d __ **Daniel** Great.
e __ **Daniel** Come on. It's my birthday.

3a Complete the conversations. Use the words in the boxes.

1 you can't ~~to~~

A We're off _to_ the pub. Are you coming?
B No, sorry. I ________.
A Oh, OK. See ________ later.

2 for you off

A I'm ________ to the café. Are ________ coming?
B Yes, OK, but only ________ a few minutes.
A Great.

b Write new conversations. Use the cues.

1 We / café / No

A [1]________ off to [2]________ ________.
Are [3]________ ________?
B No, [4]________. I [5]________.
A Oh, [6]________. See [7]________.

✓ **Now ...** ***practise and learn.***

2 I / The Coffee Shop / Yes

A [1]________________. [2]________________?
B Yes, [3]________________.
A [4]________________.

✓ **Now ...** ***practise and learn.***

Lessons 17–20

Choose the correct words and re-write the conversation.

1 **A** Hello. Can I *have / help* you? **A** ________________
2 **B** Yes. How much are *that / those* bags, please? **B** ________________
3 **A** The bags *front / in front of* the window? **A** ________________
4 **B** No, the bags next to the *boxs / boxes.* **B** ________________
5 **A** *It's / They're* £26. **A** ________________
6 **B** Can I *have / help* this one, please? **B** ________________
7 **A** *That's / It's* £26, then, please. **A** ________________
8 **B** *Here you are. / Please.* **B** ________________
9 **A** Thank you. That's £4 *change / please.* **A** ________________

✓ **Now ...** ***review your progress.***

21 Food and drinks
Pronunciation: voiced and voiceless consonants

1 Complete the table. Use the words in the box.

~~meat~~	~~tea~~	apples	wine	milk	noodles	vegetables
fish	coffee	orange juice	cheese	beer	bread	water eggs

Food	Drinks
meat	*tea*
______	______
______	______
______	______
______	______
______	______
______	______
______	

2 Label the picture.

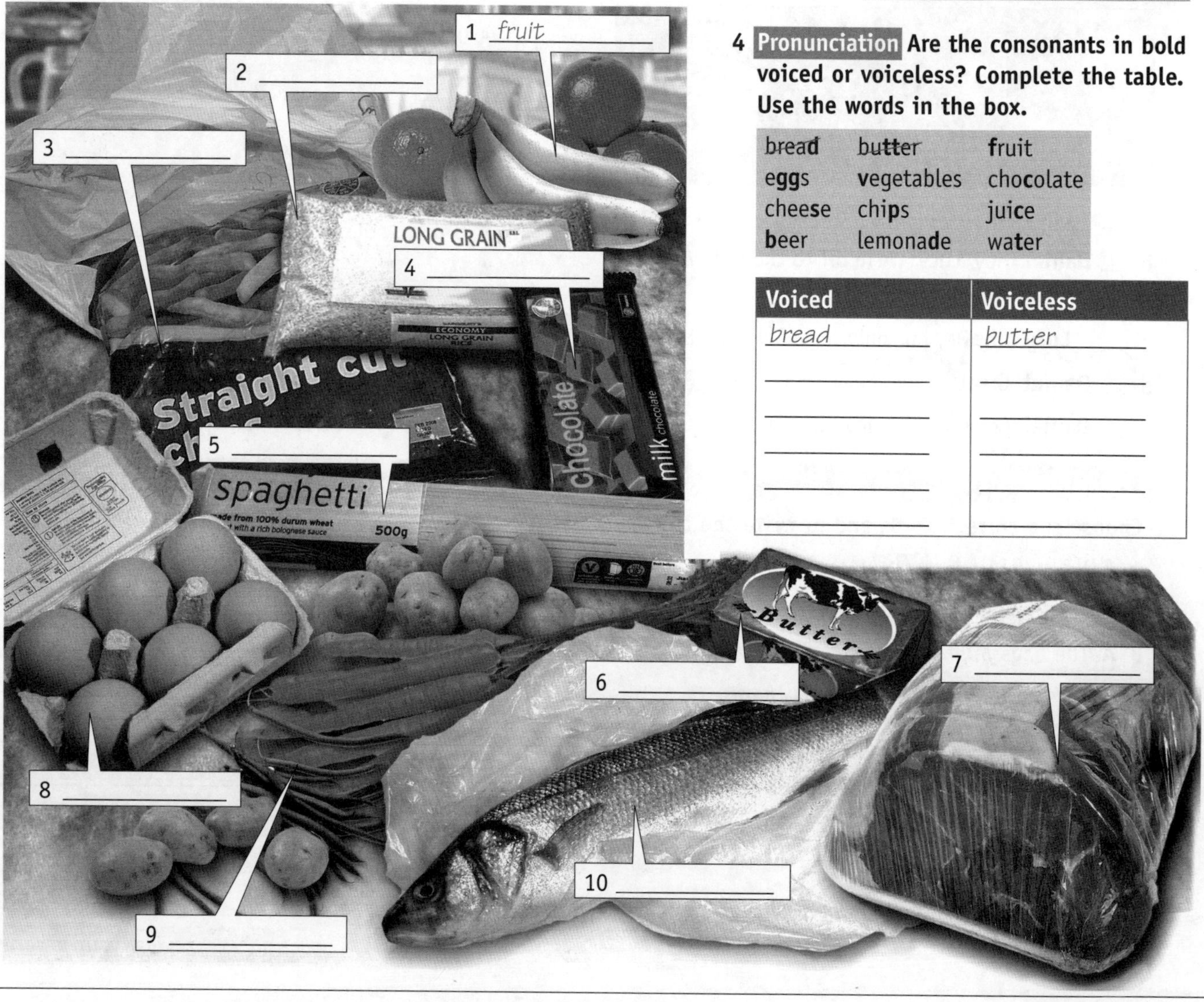

3 Complete the sentences about yourself.

1 My two favourite kinds of food are ______ and ______.

2 My two favourite drinks are ______ and ______.

3 Popular foods in my country are ______ and ______.

4 Popular drinks in my country are ______ and ______.

✓ Now ... *practise and learn.*

4 Pronunciation Are the consonants in bold voiced or voiceless? Complete the table. Use the words in the box.

~~**b**read~~	~~bu**tt**er~~	**f**ruit
e**gg**s	**v**egetables	cho**c**olate
chee**s**e	chi**p**s	jui**c**e
beer	lemona**d**e	wa**t**er

Voiced	Voiceless
bread	*butter*
______	______
______	______
______	______
______	______
______	______

22 Present simple: statements
Writing: family habits

1 Put the words in the correct order to make sentences.

1 like chocolate I

I like chocolate. ______

2 fish don't we eat

______

3 they fruit like

______

4 don't I beer drink

______

5 rice they eat

______

6 cheese we like don't

______

7 like I fruit

______

8 tea don't they drink

______

2 Make the sentences negative.

1 They drink milk.

They don't drink milk. ______

2 I like this restaurant.

______

3 We eat apples and oranges.

______

4 You drink wine.

______

5 We like cheese sandwiches.

______

6 They drink tea in the morning.

______

7 I like sport.

______

8 They eat meat.

______

3 Make sentences. Use the cues.

1 I *drink tea*,
but I *don't drink*
coffee. (drink)

2 They ______,
but they ______
______. (eat)

3 We ______,
but we ______
______. (like)

4 They ______,
but they ______
______. (drink)

5 We ______,
but we ______
______. (eat)

6 I ______,
but I ______
______. (like)

4 Write about your family.

In my family, we like ______,
but we don't like ______.
We eat ______ and ______,
but we don't eat ______.
At home, we drink ______
and ______,
but we don't drink ______.

✓ Now ... *practise and learn.*

23 Reading: meals
Writing: your eating habits

1a Solve the anagrams and write the words in the grid.

aberd	soptotae	merca
tebrut	knechic	puso
hescee	hsfi	tame

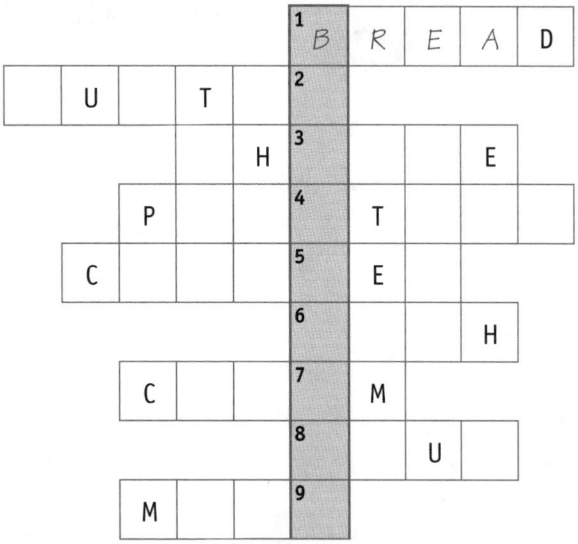

b Find the hidden word.

The hidden word is

1 B 2 ___ 3 ___ 4 ___ 5 ___ 6 ___ 7 ___ 8 ___ 9 ___.

2 Make sentences. Use the cues with *but*.

1 eat fruit / not eat apples

I *eat fruit, but I don't eat apples*.

2 not drink coffee / drink tea

We ______________________________.

3 eat bananas / not eat oranges

They ______________________________.

4 not drink milk / drink water

We ______________________________.

5 like meat / not like fish

They ______________________________.

6 eat lunch / not eat breakfast

I ______________________________.

3 Read the text. Label the pictures. Use the words in the box.

For breakfast I have two eggs with bread and butter. I drink tea.

I have my lunch at quarter past one, but I don't eat a lot – just soup and a sandwich. I drink orange juice with that.

Dinner in the evening is my big meal. I have meat with potatoes and vegetables. I drink wine with my dinner. For dessert I have fruit and cream.

breakfast lunch ~~dinner~~ dessert

1 *dinner*

2 ______________

3 ______________

4 ______________

4 Write about your meals. Complete the sentences.

For breakfast, I have ______________________________

and I drink ______________________________.

I eat ______________________________ for lunch,

and I drink ______________________________.

For dinner, I eat ______________________________

and I drink ______________________________.

✓ Now ... *practise and learn.*

24 Offering a drink
Review: lessons 21–24

1 Complete the labels.

1 w_a_t_e_r_

2 a c____

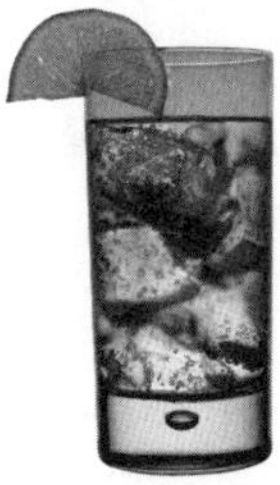

3 a g____ss

4 i____

5 a l______n

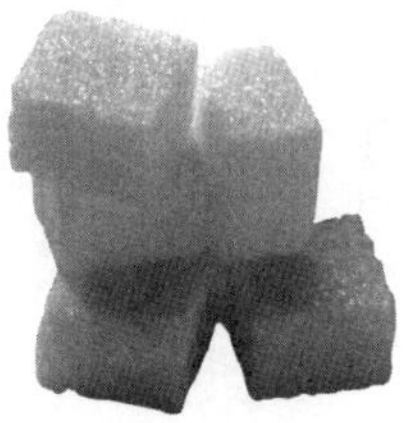

6 __u____r

2 Match the responses with the questions.

1 Ice and lemon? _e_
2 Sugar? __
3 Milk and sugar? __
4 Would you like milk or lemon in your tea? __
5 Here's your coffee. Milk or cream? __

a Just milk, please.
b Lemon, please.
c Just one, please.
d Cream, please.
e Just lemon, please. No ice.

3a Complete the conversation. Use the words in the box.

please welcome ~~like~~ are thank

A Would you [1] ___like___ a cup of coffee?
B Yes, [2] ________.
A Sugar?
B No, [3] ________ you.
A Here you [4] ________.
B Thank you.
A You're [5] ________.

b Make a new conversation.

A [1] ________ ________ ________ a cup of tea?
B Yes, [2] ________.
A Milk?
B Yes, [3] ________.
A Here [4] ________ ________.
B [5] ________ you.
A [6] ________ ________.

Lessons 21–24

Choose the correct sentences.

1 a We eat coffee.
  b We drink coffee.
2 a I no like meat.
  b I don't like meat.
3 a We eat fruit.
  b We fruit eat.
4 a Coffee they don't drink.
  b They don't drink coffee.
5 a Would you like a glass of wine?
  b Would you like a glass wine?
6 a We have coffee on breakfast.
  b We have coffee for breakfast.
7 a For lunch I have a sandwich.
  b For lunch I have sandwich.
8 a You like a cup of coffee?
  b Would you like a cup of coffee?

✓ **Now ...** *review your progress.*

25 Free-time activities
too and *either*

1 Label the pictures.

the radio, football, music, tennis, ~~shopping~~, swimming, TV, karate, novels

1 go *shopping*

2 go ________

3 watch ________

4 do ________

5 read ________

6 listen to ________

7 listen to ________

8 play ________

9 play ________

2 Complete the sentences. Use the correct verbs.

1 In my free time? Well, I *watch* TV and I ________ music. I ________ a lot of novels and I ________ yoga, too.

2 In my free time I ________ football. I ________ swimming with my children a lot. My wife and I ________ to the cinema, too.

3 Free time? Well, I ________ the radio, I ________ DVDs and I ________ computer games. Oh, and I ________ karate, too.

4 In my free time I ________ shopping and I ________ magazines. I ________ aerobics at the sports centre and I ________ tennis, too.

3 Complete the sentences. Use *too* or *either*.

1 **A** I don't play tennis.
B I don't play tennis, *either*.

2 **A** They like sport.
B We like sport, *too*.

3 **A** We go to the cinema a lot.
B I go to the cinema a lot, ________.

4 **A** I don't read newspapers.
B We don't read newspapers, ________.

5 **A** I listen to a lot of music.
B I listen to a lot of music, ________.

6 **A** We don't play computer games.
B I don't play computer games, ________.

7 **A** They go swimming.
B I go swimming, ________.

8 **A** I don't watch TV.
B We don't watch TV, ________.

4 Complete the sentences about yourself.

I *play* tennis. or I *don't play* tennis.

I ________ tennis.
I ________ TV.
I ________ to the cinema a lot.
I ________ karate.
I ________ computer games.
I ________ magazines.
I ________ swimming.
I ________ a lot of music.
I ________ novels.
I ________ aerobics.
I ________ yoga.
I ________ DVDs.
I ________ a newspaper.
I ________ go shopping a lot.

✓ **Now ...** *practise and learn.*

26 Present simple: questions
Computers

1 Make questions. Use the cues and the words in the box.

DVDs	fish	swimming	a newspaper	~~tennis~~
tea	music	the radio	computer games	karate

1 you / play

Do you play tennis?

2 you / like

____

3 you / go

____

4 you / listen to

____

5 you / eat

____

6 you / do

____

7 you / read

____

8 you / watch

____

9 you / drink

____

10 you / play

____

2 Complete the short answers.

1 Do you like football?
Yes, I *do*.

2 Do they go swimming?
No, they *don't*.

3 Do you play any sports?
No, we ________.

4 Do they watch TV in the evening?
Yes, they ________.

5 Do you read novels?
Yes, I ________.

6 Do you drink coffee?
No, we ________.

3a Make questions with *you*.

b Make short answers about yourself.

1 **A** *Do you* play sports?
You *Yes, I do.* or *No, I don't.*

2 **A** ____________ drink milk?
You ______________________________

3 **A** ____________ go swimming?
You ______________________________

4 **A** ____________ eat with chopsticks?
You ______________________________

5 **A** ____________ read computer magazines?
You ______________________________

6 **A** ____________ listen to music?
You ______________________________

✓ **Now ...** ***practise and learn.***

4 What are these parts of a computer? Solve the anagrams and complete the words.

1 a skid — a d *i s k*
2 a sorruc — a c___s___
3 a somue — a __o___e
4 a ceners — a s___e___
5 a troonim — a __o___t___
6 a brekaydo — a ___y______d

27 Reading and writing: free-time activities
Pronunciation: short and long vowels

1 Read the interview. Tick (✓) the correct boxes in the survey.

Interviewer What are your names, please?
Alicia Our names are Alicia and Manuel Moreno.
Interviewer Do you listen to the radio?
Alicia Yes, we do. We listen to the news in the morning on Radio 4.
Interviewer Do you read a newspaper?
Manuel Yes, we do. We read *The Times*.
Interviewer Thank you. And do you watch the news on TV?
Alicia Yes, we do. We watch it every day.
Interviewer Do you watch sport on TV?
Manuel No, we don't.
Interviewer Do you go to a sports centre?
Manuel Yes, we do. We go swimming there.
Interviewer And do you play any sports?
Alicia Yes, we do.
Interviewer Do you go to the cinema?
Alicia Yes, we do.
Interviewer OK. Do you play computer games?
Manuel No, we don't. We don't like them.
Interviewer Thank you very much.

What do you do in your free time?

Name *Alicia and Manuel Moreno*

Do you ...?	**Yes**	**No**
1 listen to the radio	✓	
2 read a newspaper		
3 watch the news on TV		
4 watch sport on TV		
5 go to a sports centre		
6 play any sports		
7 go to the cinema		
8 play computer games		

2 Complete the interview about yourself.

Interviewer What's your name, please?
You My name's ______________________.
Interviewer Do you listen to the radio?
You ______________________
Interviewer Do you read a newspaper?
You ______________________
Interviewer Thank you. And do you watch the news on TV?
You ______________________
Interviewer Do you watch sport on TV?
You ______________________
Interviewer Do you go to a sports centre?
You ______________________
Interviewer Do you play any sports?
You Sports? ______________________
Interviewer Do you go to the cinema?
You ______________________
Interviewer OK. Do you play computer games?
You ______________________
Interviewer Thank you.

✓ Now ... *practise and learn.*

3 Pronunciation Are the vowel sounds short or long? Complete the table. Use the words in the box.

car **kar**ate you **nov**el ~~drink~~
cat purse sport eat good

Short vowels		Long vowels	
/ɪ/	**lis**ten *drink*	/iː/	read __________
/ɒ/	**coff**ee __________	/ɔː/	**morn**ing __________
/ʊ/	**sug**ar __________	/uː/	two __________
/æ/	man __________	/ɑː/	glass __________
/ə/	chil**dren** __________	/ɜː/	girl __________

28 Offering a lift
Review: lessons 25–28

1 Match the bubbles with the pictures.

1 I'm going to the shops. _d_

2 I'm going to Paris. __

3 I'm going to the sports centre. __

4 I'm going to a meeting. __

a

b

c

d

2 Number the conversation in the correct order.

a __ **Kamran** Would you like a lift?
b __ **Rico** Oh hello, Kamran. I'm fine, thanks.
c __ **Rico** Yes, please.
d _1_ **Kamran** Hi Rico. How are you?
e __ **Kamran** Where are you off to?
f __ **Rico** I'm going to the cinema.

3 Complete the conversation. Use the words in the box.

I'm to lift ~~off~~

Bill Morning, Emma. Where are you [1]_off_ to?
Emma [2]________ going to the sports centre. And you?
Bill I'm going [3]________ a meeting at Marco's office.
Emma Oh. That's next to the sports centre. Would you like a [4]________?
Bill Yes, please.

4 Complete the sign.

P__V__E
N_ P__K__G

Lessons 25–28

Complete the sentences.

1 I ____________ tennis on Sundays.
2 ____________ you like sport?
3 I'm going ____________ a meeting.
4 'Do they go shopping on Saturdays?'
'Yes, they ____________.'
5 We ____________ swimming at the weekend.
6 I ____________ aerobics at the sports centre.
7 Would you ____________ a lift?
8 'Do you enjoy computer games?'
'No, I ____________.'

✓ **Now ...** *review your progress.*

29 Describing where you live and work

1 Choose the correct sentences to match the pictures.

1 a I live in a town. ✓
b I live in a village.

2 a I work in a restaurant.
b I work in a factory.

3 a I live in a house.
b I live in a flat.

4 a I work in a hospital.
b I work in a bank.

5 a I drive to work.
b I walk to work.

6 a I live alone.
b I live with my family.

2 Complete the table. Use the words and expressions in the box.

a small town	~~alone~~	take the bus	walk
with my parents	school	the suburbs	flat

I live ...	___alone___, with two friends, with my family, ______.
I live in a ...	house, ______.
My home is in ...	the city centre, ______, a village, ______.
I ...	______, drive, ______, take the metro ...
... to ...	work, ______, university.

3 Complete the texts. Use the words in the boxes.

1 flat walk ~~alone~~ centre

2 house drive family suburbs

4 Write about yourself.

I live ______________________.
I live in ______________________
My home is in ______________________.
I ______________ to ______________.

✓ **Now ...** ***practise and learn.***

30 Present simple: *wh-* questions
Writing: your everyday life

1 Match the questions with the answers.

1 a Where do your parents live? *i* — i In the suburbs.
b Do your parents live in a house? *ii* — ii No, they don't.

2 a Do you live alone? ___ — i In the city centre.
b Where do you live? ___ — ii Yes, I do.

3 a What do you do in your free time? ___ — i We play tennis.
b Do you play tennis? ___ — ii Yes, we do.

4 a Where do they do aerobics? ___ — i At the sports centre.
b Do they play any sports? ___ — ii No, they don't.

5 a Do they drive to work? ___ — i By car.
b How do you go to work? ___ — ii Yes, they do.

6 a What newspaper do you read? ___ — i I don't read a newspaper.
b Do you read a newspaper? ___ — ii No, I don't.

7 a Do you like sport? ___ — i We play football.
b What sports do you play? ___ — ii Yes, we do.

8 a When do you have lunch? ___ — i At one o'clock.
b Do you have lunch at one o'clock? ___ — ii No, we don't.

2 Make questions. Put the words and phrases in the correct order.

1 go swimming do you when ?
When do you go swimming?

2 have what time they dinner do ?
____

3 where tennis they play do ?
____

4 go to school how do you ?
____

5 for breakfast eat what you do ?
____

6 where you do lunch have ?
____

7 in your free time do you what do ?
____

8 open do the shops what time ?
____

3 Complete the questions. Use the answers to help you.

1 **A** Where *do* *you live*?
B I live in a flat.

2 **A** Who ______ ______ with?
B I live with my wife and children.

3 **A** Where ______ ______?
B I work in a bank.

4 **A** How ______ ______ to work?
B I walk to work.

5 **A** What time ______ ______ lunch?
B At half past one.

6 **A** What ______ in the evening?
B We watch TV.

7 **A** When ______ ______ shopping?
B At the weekend.

4 Give your own answers to the questions in exercise 3.

1 ______________________
2 ______________________
3 ______________________
4 ______________________
5 ______________________
6 ______________________
7 ______________________

✓ **Now ...** ***practise and learn.***

31 Reading: lifestyles
Addresses

1 Read the conversation. Tick (✓) the things that the interviewer asks about.

their names ✓	their home	holidays
work	free time	books

Interviewer What's your name?
Angela My name's Angela and my husband's name is Michael.
Interviewer Where do you live?
Angela We live in Dublin.
Interviewer Do you like Dublin?
Angela Yes, we do. It's a great city.
Interviewer Do you live in the city centre?
Angela Yes, we do. We live in a flat there.
Interviewer Do you work in the city, too?
Angela Yes, we do. We work at the university.
Interviewer Do you walk to work?
Angela Yes, we do. It's in the city centre, too.
Interviewer What do you do in your free time?
Angela We run in marathons.
Interviewer Really?
Angela Yes, we love it.
Interviewer What other things do you do?
Angela Well, we like music, so we go to concerts a lot.

2 Choose the correct words and phrases.

1 They *like* / ~~*don't like*~~ Dublin.
2 They live in the *suburbs* / *city centre*.
3 They live in a *house* / *flat*.
4 They work *at the university* / *in offices*.
5 They *drive* / *walk* to work.
6 In their free time they *run in marathons* / *go swimming*.
7 They love *marathons* / *university*.
8 They go to *the cinema* / *concerts* a lot.

3 Write the places in full.

1 Factory Rd. Factory Road
2 Oxford St. ______
3 West Ave. ______
4 City Rd. ______

4 Write the addresses. Use short forms.

1
What's your address?
It's seventy-five Factory Road.

75 Factory Rd.

2
My address is ten Ash Street.

______

3
I live at sixty China Avenue.

______

4
My office is eighty South Road.

______

5 Write the names and addresses on the envelopes.

1 M6 8LV Manchester
~~Mr Winston Deane~~ East Rd. 15

Mr Winston Deane
______
______
______

2 Cambridge 87 Ms I. Lovett
CB9 4RT London St.

______
______
______
______

32 Days and times; punctuation
Review: lessons 29–32

1 Complete the days in the diary.

M _o_ _n_ **day**	**T**____**d**___	___**d**____**day**	**T**______**day**
___**i**___**y**	**S**____**r**____	___**n**____	

2 Write the sentences. Use the correct punctuation and capital letters.

1 **A** is annas party on friday
Is Anna's party on Friday?
B no it isnt
____

2 **A** what times your appointment at the doctors
____
____
B its at two oclock
____

3 **A** wheres suchart from
____
B hes from thailand
____

4 **A** whens johans driving test
____
B its on tuesday
____

3 Complete the sentences. Use *on* or *at*.

1 **A** What day is your interview?
B It's _on_ Monday.

2 **A** Do you play football _____ the weekend?
B No, we don't. We play _____ Thursdays.

3 **A** Is your party _____ Saturday?
B Yes, it is. It's _____ half past two.

4 **A** Is the bank open _____ the weekend?
B It's open _____ Saturday, but it's closed _____ Sunday.

5 **A** What time is our meeting _____ Friday?
B It's _____ 2.15.

6 **A** Is your appointment _____ ten o'clock?
B No, it isn't. It's _____ eleven.

Lessons 29–32

Choose the correct sentences.

1 a I live in a flat.
b I live at a flat.

2 a We walk in a restaurant.
b We work in a restaurant.

3 a Do you drive to work?
b Do you drive to the work?

4 a Where you live?
b Where do you live?

5 a Where do you do in your free time?
b What do you do in your free time?

6 a My appointment is at Monday.
b My appointment is on Monday.

7 a What day is it today?
b What day is today?

8 a Is your meeting on Tuesday?
b Is your meeting on tuesday?

✓ **Now ...** ***review your progress.***

Daily activities

1a Match the pictures with the activities.

Lanisha's day

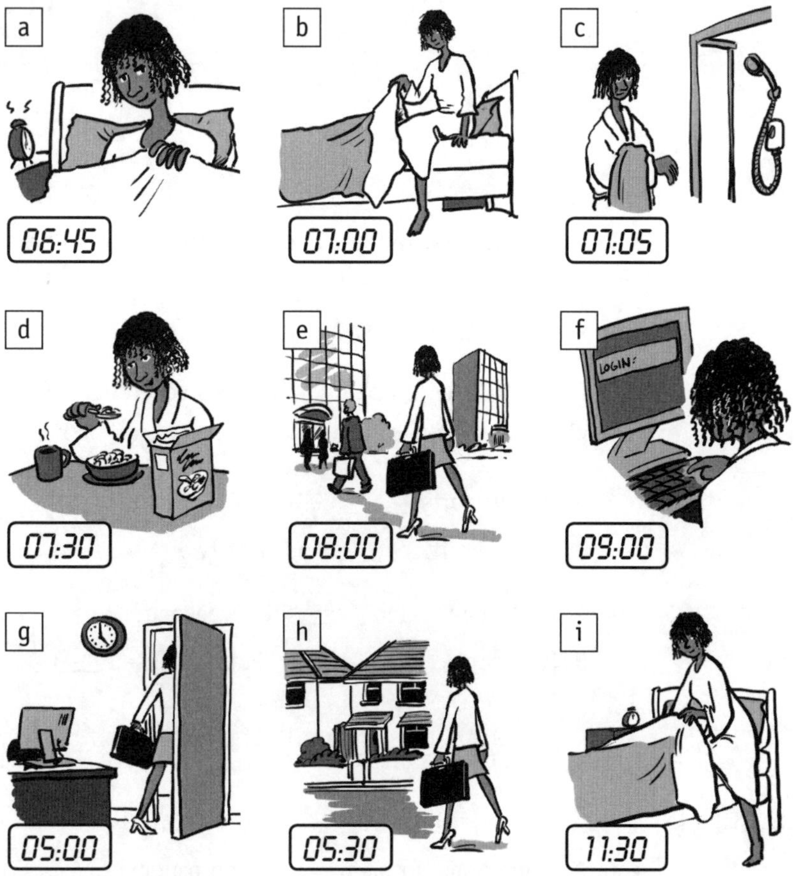

1 go to bed _i_
2 wake up __
3 go to work __
4 have a shower __
5 go home __
6 have breakfast __
7 start work __
8 get up __
9 finish work __

b Complete Lanisha's sentences about her day.

1 I ___wake up___ at 6.45.
2 I ______________ at seven o'clock.
3 I ______________ at 7.05.
4 I ______________ 7.30.
5 I ______________ at eight o'clock.
6 I ______________ at nine o'clock.
7 I ______________ at five o'clock.
8 I ______________ at 5.30.
9 I ______________ at 11.30.

2 Answer the questions about yourself.

1 What time do you wake up?
I ___wake up___ at ______________.
2 What time do you get up?
I ______________ at ______________.
3 What time do you have breakfast?
I ______________ at ______________.
4 What time do you go to work or school?
I ______________ at ______________.
5 What time do you start work or school?
I ______________ at ______________.
6 What time do you have lunch?
I ______________ at ______________.
7 What time do you finish work or school?
I ______________ at ______________.
8 What time do you go to bed?
I ______________ at ______________.
9 What time do you get up at the weekend?
I ______________ at ______________.

✓ Now ... *practise and learn.*

3 What is a typical working day in your country?

a Write the times for the activities.

______________ eat breakfast
______________ start work
______ – ______ have a tea / coffee break
______________ eat lunch
______ – ______ have a tea / coffee break
______________ finish work
______________ eat dinner

b Which is the big meal of the day?

____

34 Present simple: third person singular
Pronunciation: present simple *-es* endings

1 Make sentences about Miroslav's life.

1 I share a flat with two friends.
He *shares* a flat with two friends.
2 I work in a factory.
He ____________ in a factory.
3 I watch TV in the evening.
He ____________ TV in the evening.
4 I play computer games, too.
He ____________ computer games, too.
5 I do karate.
He ____________ karate.
6 I go swimming on Saturdays.
He ____________ swimming on Saturdays.

2 Make the sentences about Bella negative.

1 Bella lives alone.
Bella *doesn't live* alone.
2 She works in a hospital.
She ____________ in a hospital.
3 She starts work at 8.30.
She ____________ at 8.30.
4 She has lunch at a restaurant.
She ____________ at a restaurant.
5 She finishes work at 5.15.
She ____________ at 5.15.
6 She does yoga in her free time.
She ____________ in her free time.

3 Choose the correct words.

1 I *work* / ~~*works*~~ in a shop.
2 She *work* / *works* in a hospital.
3 He *live* / *lives* in a flat.
4 They *go* / *goes* hang-gliding.
5 We *play* / *plays* football.
6 He *finish* / *finishes* work at 6.30.
7 She *do* / *does* aerobics.
8 I *get up* / *gets up* at 7.15.
9 We *take* / *takes* the bus to school.
10 He *drive* / *drives* to work.

4 Complete the sentences. Use *don't* or *doesn't*.

1 I *don't* like my boss.
2 She ____________ eat breakfast.
3 Ben ____________ go to work.
4 We ____________ watch a lot of DVDs.
5 He ____________ smoke.
6 My parents ____________ live near here.
7 My friend ____________ drink coffee or tea.
8 I ____________ drive to work.

5a Pronunciation How many syllables? Write the number in the brackets.

b Tick (✓) the verbs with an extra syllable in the *-s/-es* form.

	Verb (*I / You / We / They*)	Verb + *-s / -es* (*He / She / It*)	Extra syllable?
1	drive (1)	drives (*1*)	
2	finish (2)	finishes (*3*)	✓
3	do (1)	does (__)	
4	go (1)	goes (__)	
5	use (1)	uses (__)	
6	live (1)	lives (__)	
7	watch (1)	watches (__)	
8	take (1)	takes (__)	

35 Reading: a description of someone's daily life
Prepositions of time

1 Read the first paragraph of the text. Choose the correct alternatives.

1 Elsa Martin lives in *South Africa / Australia*.
2 She lives *with her husband / alone*.
3 She lives in a *city / town*.
4 She's a *doctor / medical assistant*.
5 She works in a *hospital / health centre*.
6 The centre is for *men / children*.

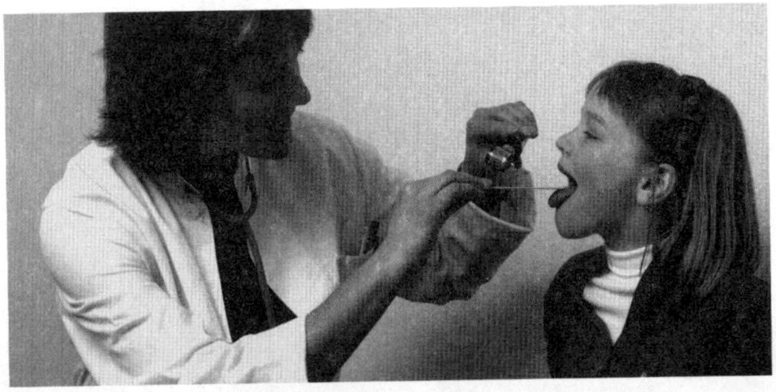

Elsa Martin lives in Australia. She lives with her husband in a town near the city of Perth. Elsa is a doctor and she works in a children's health centre.

Her day starts at five o'clock in the morning. She gets up, has a shower and gets dressed. Then she has breakfast and watches TV.

At half past six she goes to work. She drives to the health centre. It takes half an hour. She starts work at seven o'clock and she finishes work at three o'clock in the afternoon. She goes home at 3.30 p.m. Her husband, Luke, comes home at six o'clock and they have dinner at 6.15.

On Wednesdays, Elsa doesn't go to the health centre. She drives to the villages in her district. Some of the villages are a hundred kilometres away, but the roads are good. She visits people in their homes. She visits 10–15 families in a day. She goes home at six o'clock in the evening.

2 Read the full text. Are the statements true (T) or false (F)?

1 _T_ Elsa is married.
2 ___ She listens to the radio in the morning.
3 ___ She takes the bus to work.
4 ___ She goes to the health centre every weekday.
5 ___ On Wednesdays she visits families in their homes.
6 ___ She goes to the villages on a motorbike.
7 ___ The roads in the district are good.
8 ___ She visits twenty families in a day.

3 What happens at these times? Complete the sentences.

1 She __gets up__ at five o'clock in the morning.
2 She ________ at half past six.
3 She ________ at seven o'clock.
4 She ________ at three o'clock.
5 She ________ at half past three.
6 She ________ at quarter past six.

4a Complete the table. Use the words in the box.

quarter to four	Monday	~~the evening~~
Wednesday	10.25	the morning

in **+ parts of the day**	the evening the afternoon ________
on **+ days**	Sunday ________ Friday ________
at **+ times**	two o'clock ________ 7.30 ________

b Complete the sentences about Elsa. Use *in*, *on* or *at*.

1 Elsa gets up __at__ five o'clock ________ the morning.
2 She works ________ the afternoon.
3 She visits one village ________ the morning and one village ________ the afternoon.
4 She doesn't work ________ Saturdays.
5 Elsa and Luke have dinner ________ 6.15 ________ the evening.
6 They go shopping ________ Saturday.

36 Problems
Review: lessons 33–36

1 Number the parts of the story in the correct order.

a ___ Lucy sees a note on her car. It's from Jordan.

b ___ Lucy goes to Jordan's office. She says sorry.

c _1_ Lucy parks in Jordan's private parking space.

d ___ Lucy drives to Cambridge, but the meeting is over. Lucy's in trouble.

e ___ Jordan parks his van behind Lucy's car.

2 Complete the conversation. Put the words in brackets in the correct order.

Mrs King Hello, Danny, how are you?

Danny Fine, thanks, Mrs King, but [1] _I'm in a hurry_ (hurry I'm a in). It's ten o'clock and [2] ______________ (late a lesson for I'm). The teacher is Mr Fury, too. He doesn't like me.

Mrs King Oh, well, would you like a lift?

Danny Yes, please, Mrs King.

LATER

Mr Fury OK, class. See you tomorrow. ... Danny! It's half past ten! The lesson is over. [3] ______________ (terrible this is).

Danny Oh no! [4] ______________ (trouble in I'm) now.

Lessons 33–36

Correct the mistakes.

1 I gets up at 7.15.
I ______________ at 7.15.

2 She work in a hospital.
She ______________ in a hospital.

3 He gos to school.
He ______________ to school.

4 We has dinner at 6.30.
We ______________ dinner at 6.30.

5 She don't like coffee.
She ______________ coffee.

6 I doesn't play football.
I ______________ football.

7 He doesn't watches TV.
He ______________ TV.

8 I work at the evening.
I work ______________ the evening.

✓ **Now ...** ***review your progress.***

37 Jobs
Asking and answering about jobs

1 Complete the jobs.

1 s____re___ary
2 w_______er
3 ___ur___e
4 c_____f
5 bu_____d___r
6 sh_____ as___is_______t
7 ho_______w___f___
8 m___ch_______c
9 t_____ch_____
10 st___d_______
11 w_____t_____ss
12 com_____t___r en_____ne___r

2 Complete the crossword. The answers are all jobs in exercise 1.

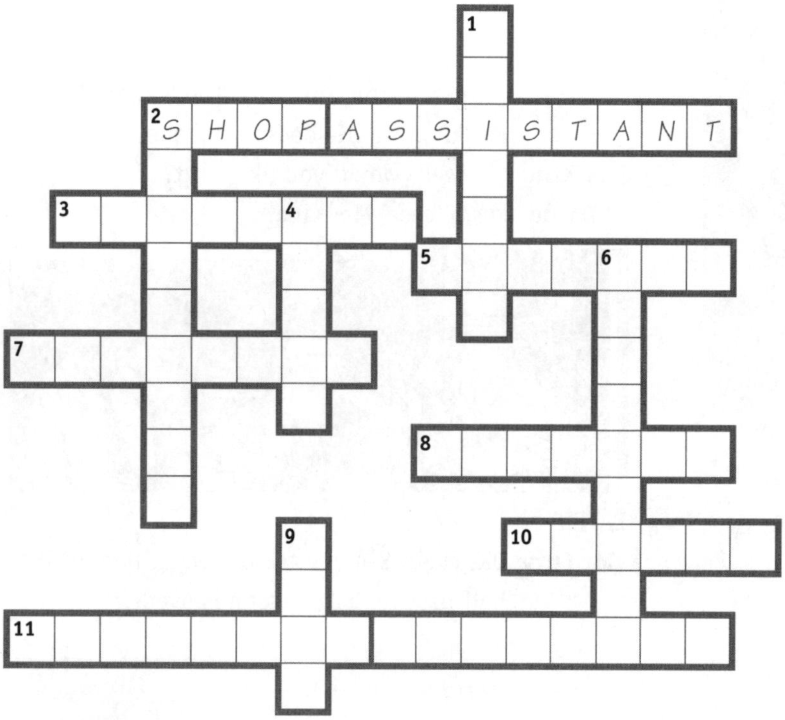

Across

2 This person sells things in a shop.
3 This person fixes machines.
5 This person teaches in a school.
7 This woman serves food and drinks in a restaurant.
8 This person goes to university.
10 This man serves food and drinks in a restaurant.
11 This person fixes computers.

Down

1 This person builds houses.
2 This person types letters in an office.
4 This person looks after people in hospital.
6 This woman works at home and looks after her family.
9 This person cooks food in a restaurant.

3 Write your job and the jobs of five people that you know (members of your family, friends, neighbours).

1 I'm ____________________.
2 My __________ is ___________.
3 My ____________________.
4 My ____________________.
5 My ____________________.

4a Complete the conversation. Use the words in the box.

where a teach what ~~do~~

A What [1] *do* you do?
B I'm [2]__________ teacher.
A [3]__________ do you work?
B I work in a school in the city centre.
A [4]__________ do you teach?
B I [5]__________ French.

b Write a conversation about your life.

A What ________ you ________?
You I'm ____________________.
A ________________ you work?
You I ________ in ____________.
A What do you do there?
You I ____________________
____________________.

✓ Now ... *practise and learn.*

38 Present simple: questions

1 Complete the sentences. Use *do* or *does*.

1 Where ___do___ you work?

2 ________ they live near here?

3 What ________ John do?

4 ________ he like his job?

5 ________ you like your boss?

6 ________ Lucy work at weekends?

7 What ________ you do in your free time?

8 How ________ you go to work?

2 Complete the short answers.

1 **A** Does Maria like her job?
B Yes, she ___does___.

2 **A** Do you work in a bank?
B No, I ____________.

3 **A** Do they finish work at 5.30?
B Yes, ____________.

4 **A** Do you play computer games?
B No, we ____________.

5 **A** Does Pedro live with his parents?
B No, ____________.

6 **A** Does Anna drive to work?
B Yes, ____________.

7 **A** Do you live near the sports centre?
B Yes, we ____________.

8 **A** Does Sarah want a lift?
B No, ____________.

9 **A** Do Carmen and Alejandro like chocolate?
B No, ____________.

10 **A** Do you work at home?
B Yes, I ____________.

3 Complete the conversation. Make questions. Use the cues.

1 **A** Where / your daughter / live?
Where does your daughter live?
B She lives in Brussels.

2 **A** What / she / do?
____
B She's a nurse.

3 **A** she / work / in a hospital?
____
B Yes, she does.

4 **A** Where / they / live?
____
B They live in a house in the suburbs.

5 **A** they / like / Brussels?
____
B Yes, they do. They love it there.

4a Answer the questions about yourself.

b Answer the questions about a member of your family.

1 What do you do?
I'm a ____________________.
He's/She's a ____________________.

2 Where do you work/study?
____
____

3 Do you drive to work/school/university?
____
____

4 What time do you start?
____
____

5 When do you finish?
____
____

6 Do you like your job/studies?
____
____

✓ **Now ...** *practise and learn.*

39 Reading: jobs and ambitions
Pronunciation: schwa /ə/

1 Read the text about Antonio's day. Choose the correct answers.

1 Antonio gets up at
   a two o'clock in the morning. ✓
   b two o'clock in the afternoon.
   c five o'clock in the evening.

2 He works at
   a a hospital.
   b a newspaper.
   c a radio station.

3 His job is
   a working on the breakfast programme.
   b cooking breakfast for the newsreaders.
   c cleaning the radio station offices.

4 He wants to work
   a for a newspaper.
   b in films.
   c for a TV company.

2a Complete the questions in b.

b Read the text again and answer the questions.

1 _What_ does Antonio do?
   He's a _radio newsreader_ ________.
2 ________ does he go to work?
   He ________.
3 ________ he have breakfast at home?
   ____
4 ________ does the programme start?
   It starts at ________.
5 When ________ the programme finish?
   It ________.
6 Does he ________ home immediately?
   ____
7 ________ time does he go home?
   He ________.
8 What does he ________ in his free time?
   He ________ and he ________.
9 What days ________ he work?
   He works from ________ to ________.
10 ________ he like his job?
   ________ he ________.

Antonio's Day

Antonio's day starts at 2 a.m. He gets up, has a shower and gets dressed. He doesn't have breakfast at home. He just drinks a cup of coffee. Then he drives to work. He works at a local radio station. He arrives at three o'clock. He has breakfast, and then he starts work. Antonio is a newsreader. His day starts very early, because he reads the news on the breakfast programme.

The programme starts at six o'clock and it finishes at nine o'clock. Antonio doesn't go home immediately. First he eats 'lunch', and then he prepares things for the next day. He goes home at 11 o'clock. In the afternoon, Antonio plays tennis. He goes to the cinema a lot, too.

Antonio doesn't work at the weekend.
The breakfast programme is on from Monday to Friday.

Does he like his job? 'I love it,' he says. 'It's very interesting and I work with some great people. I have a lot of free time, too. But I really want to work for a TV company.'

3 Pronunciation Underline the syllable with the *schwa* /ə/ sound.

1 tea<u>cher</u>
2 doctor
3 waiter
4 brother
5 newsreader
6 singer
7 reporter
8 builder

40 Getting to know someone
Review: lessons 37–40

1 Complete the conversation. Use the questions.

Do you work for the local newspaper?
What do you want to do?
~~Do you live near here~~?
Where do you live?
What do you do?
Do you like your job?
Where do you work?

Esta Hi. My name's Esta.
Ivan Pleased to meet you, Esta. I'm Ivan.
Esta Nice to meet you. [1] *Do you live near here?*
Ivan Yes, I do.
Esta Me too!
Ivan I live in Ascot Street. What about you? [2] ______
Esta I live on Marchmont Road.
Ivan Oh, right. [3] ______
Esta I'm a reporter.
Ivan Oh, I see. That's interesting. [4] ______
Esta Yes, I do – *The Echo*.
Ivan [5] ______
Esta Yes, I do. It's a very interesting job. What about you? [6] ______
Ivan In a café. I'm a waiter, but I don't like it.
Esta [7] ______
Ivan I want to be an actor.
Esta Really? I love films.

2 Are the statements true (T) or false (F)?

1 *T* Ivan lives in Ascot Street.
2 __ Esta works for the local newspaper.
3 __ She's a secretary.
4 __ Esta doesn't like her job.
5 __ Ivan works in an office.
6 __ He likes his job.
7 __ He wants to be an actor.
8 __ Esta doesn't like films.

3 Complete the expressions. Use the conversation in exercise 1 to help you.

1 O*h*, ri*gh*t.
2 M__ t____.
3 T____t's inter______ing.
4 R____lly?
5 Oh, I s____.

Lessons 37–40

Correct the mistakes.

1 What you do?
______
2 He's builder.
______
3 Do she live in a city?
______
4 Does he likes his job?
______
5 Where you live?
______
6 'Does Maria work here?' 'No, she don't.'
______
7 When does you finish work?
______
8 She want to be a singer.
______

✓ **Now ...** *review your progress.*

41 Adjectives

1 Complete the sentences. Use the words in the box.

short cold big ~~old~~ long young hot old new small

1 My car is _old_.

2 Sara drives a _____ car.

3 I like my _____ hair.

4 Jake's hair is _____.

5 Would you like a _____ drink?

6 I like _____ drinks.

7 Lisa's grandmother is an _____ woman.

8 Lisa is a _____ girl.

9 My uncle's house is _____.

10 Cristian lives in a _____ house.

2 What are the colours?

1 erd r_e_d_
2 clakb __ __ a __ __
3 lebu __ l __ __
4 groane __ __ __ __ g __
5 thewi __ h __ __ __
6 wronb __ __ __ w __
7 wolley __ __ __ __ __ w
8 reneg g __ __ __ __

3 Choose the correct sentences.

1 a That's a restaurant good.
  b That's a good restaurant. ✓
2 a I'd like a hot drink.
  b I'd like a drink hot.
3 a I play tennis with three good friends.
  b I play tennis with good friends three.
4 a How much are those reds bags?
  b How much are those red bags?
5 a That's Katrina's new boyfriend.
  b That's Katrina's boyfriend new.

4 Complete the sentences. Put the words in brackets in the correct order.

1 I like _blue cars_. (cars blue)
2 We live in _______________. (small a village)
3 This is _______________. (meal a bad)
4 I work with _______________. (two women young)
5 Don't use _______________. (pen red a)
6 He drives _______________? (a car black)
7 Is that _______________? (new a computer)
8 Would you like _______________? (drink cold a)

5 Complete the sentences about yourself. Use the correct colours.

1 My favourite colour is _______________.
2 My eyes are _______________.
3 The door of my house/flat is _______________.
4 My bag/briefcase is _______________.
5 Our English book is _______________.
6 My car is _______________.

42 *have got / has got*
Writing: your personal possessions

1 Complete the sentences. Use short forms.

1 Jordan has got a white van.
Jordan's got a white van.

2 We have got two children.
__________ two children.

3 I have not got a job.
__________ a job.

4 She has not got a meeting today.
__________ a meeting today.

5 You have got my book.
__________ my book.

6 Anan has got a nice dog.
__________ a nice dog.

7 We have not got a test now.
__________ a test now.

8 My office has not got a window.
__________ a window.

2 Make the sentences negative. Use short forms.

1 She's got an umbrella.
She hasn't got an umbrella.

2 They've got a new flat.
____

3 We've got a brown cat.
____

4 Lucy's got a good boss.
____

5 You've got my mobile number.
____

6 We've got a meeting now.
____

7 He's got an old computer.
____

8 I've got a young secretary.
____

3 Choose the correct sentences.

1 a John haven't got a computer.
b John hasn't got a computer. ✓

2 a I've a motorbike got.
b I've got a motorbike.

3 a We haven't got a car.
b We hasn't got a car.

4 a I no have got a good job.
b I haven't got a good job.

5 a He got two brothers.
b He's got two brothers.

6 a Bill and Kath have got a nice house.
b Bill and Kath has got a nice house.

7 a Sheena doesn't have got a new job.
b Sheena hasn't got a new job.

8 a Alex no has got a new mobile.
b Alex hasn't got a new mobile.

4a Has Liam got these things in his pockets?

~~an address book~~ ~~a mobile~~ a hairbrush a wallet a key a pen

1 *He hasn't got an address book.*
2 *He's got a mobile.*
3 __________
4 __________
5 __________
6 __________

b Have you got the things in your bag or pockets?

1 I __________ an address book.
2 I __________ a mobile.
3 __________
4 __________
5 __________
6 __________

43 Reading: a personal email
Text messages

1 Read the email. Choose the correct names.

1 Who is it from? Ben Tina
2 Who is it to? Ben Tina
3 Who is at university? Ben Tina

Dear Ben

Good news! I've got a new flat. It's in one of those old houses near the park.

I share the flat with three other people, but it's a very big flat and I've got my own room.

The room's small, but it's OK. I've got a bed and a desk for my computer. I haven't got a phone in my room, but it's OK, because I've got my mobile.

And I've got a private parking space for my car, too. That's great.

Anyway, I really like the flat and my flatmates are very nice. Two of them are students and the other one works for a music company.

Hope you're OK. How are things at university? Take care.

Lots of love,

Tina

PS Guess what? I've got a new boss at work. He's young, but he's very good.

2 What is the email about? Tick (✓) four things.

her new office
her new job
her new flat ✓
her new boyfriend
her new boss
her flatmates
her new car
her parking space

3 Are the statements true (T) or false (F)?

1 _F_ Tina shares the flat with two other people.
2 __ It's in a new block of flats.
3 __ The flat is very big.
4 __ She hasn't got her own room.
5 __ Her room is big.
6 __ She's got a desk in her room.
7 __ She's got a parking space.
8 __ She hasn't got a car.
9 __ Her flatmates are doctors.
10 __ She doesn't like her new boss.

4 Match the parts of the sentences.

1 The flat is _d_ a young
2 The house is __ b small
3 Her room is __ c very nice
4 The parking space is __ d very big
5 Her flatmates are __ e private
6 Her new boss is __ f old

5 Match the text messages with the correct meanings.

a how r u?
b pls txt me
c c u l8r.
d hpy bday 2 u!
e r u ok?
f hv a gd time 2nite

1 Please text me. _b_
2 How are you? __
3 Happy Birthday to you! __
4 Are you OK? __
5 Have a good time tonight. __
6 See you later. __

44 Asking for a seat
Review: lessons 41–44

1a Match the parts of the sentences.

1 Are _b_
2 There's ___
3 I'm sorry. They're ___
4 Is ___
5 Go ___

a this seat free?
b these seats free?
c ahead.
d a table over there.
e taken.

2 Write the complete expressions in the bubbles.

1
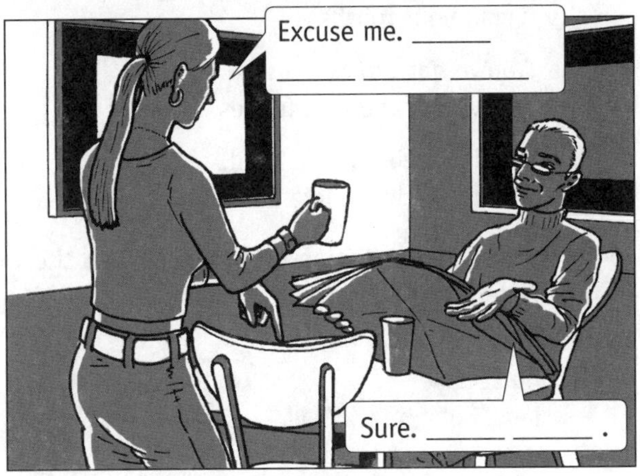

2

3 Put the words in the correct order to make sentences and questions.

1 a we've neighbour got new
We've got a new neighbour.

2 you do my friend Gita know ?
______

3 live here near you do ?
______

4 I in live flats block of a
______

5 over there my is house
______

6 Carlos hair long got hasn't
______

7 don't London work in I
______

8 Sunita got her office own has
______

9 laptop my fast really is
______

10 haven't we got new flat a
______

11 drives car Bruno old an
______

12 like you hot a would drink ?
______

Lessons 41–44

Choose the correct sentences.

1 a Carlos have got a new girlfriend.
  b Carlos has got a new girlfriend.
2 a I've got two cats white.
  b I've got two white cats.
3 a We haven't got a dog.
  b We don't have got a dog.
4 a I work in an office big.
  b I work in a big office.
5 a I've got greens eyes.
  b I've got green eyes.
6 a She no has got a car.
  b She hasn't got a car.
7 a She's got two sisters.
  b She got two sisters.
8 a Is these seats free?
  b Is this seat free?

✓ **Now ...** *review your progress.*

45 Parts of the body
Pronunciation: vowel sounds

1 Complete the picture crossword.

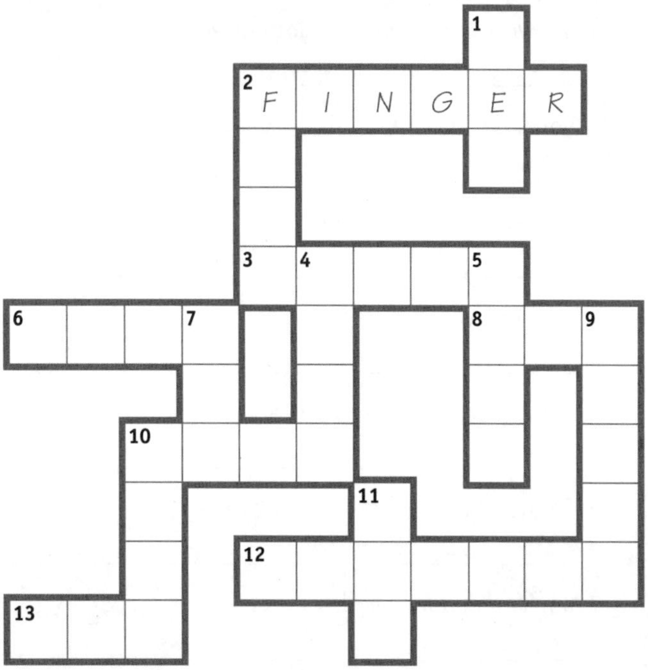

Across

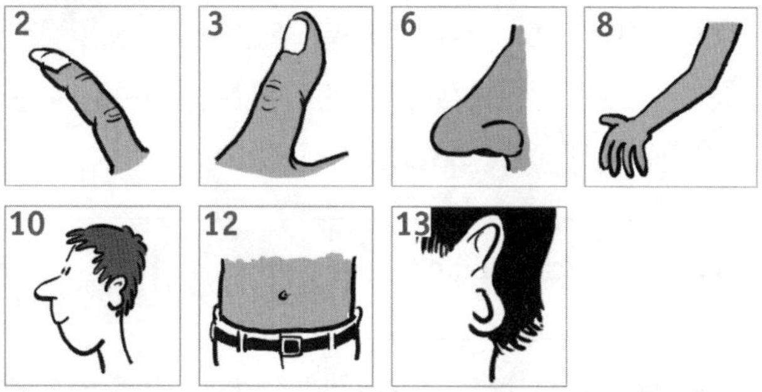

Down

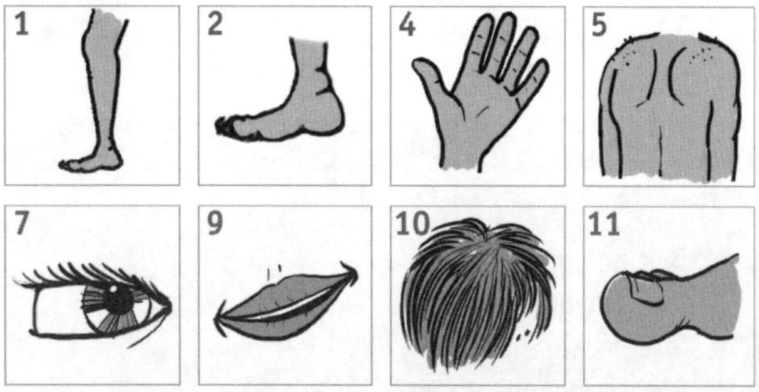

2 Choose the correct sentences.

1 a She's got hair long.
  b She's got long hair. ✓

2 a I've got big foots.
  b I've got big feet.

3 a He's got short hairs.
  b He's got short hair.

4 a Clean your teeth.
  b Clean your tooths.

5 a You've got brown eyes.
  b You've got the brown eyes.

6 a I write with my left hand.
  b I write with the left hand.

3 Write five sentences about yourself. Use the words in the box to help you.

I've got / I haven't got ...	
... big / small	hands / feet
... dark / light / black / red	hair
... brown / blue / green	eyes
... long / short	arms / legs
... a big / small	nose / mouth

1 *I've ...* ______________________

____

2 *I haven't ...* ______________________

____

3 ______________________

____

4 ______________________

5 ______________________

____

✓ **Now ...** *practise and learn.*

4 Pronunciation Tick (✓) the pairs of words with the same vowel sound.

1 hair — ear
2 back — hand ✓
3 toe — nose
4 tooth — mouth
5 hand — arm
6 head — leg
7 thumb — **stom**ach
8 feet — eye

46 *have got / has got*: questions
Writing: describing your possessions

1 Put the words and phrases in the correct order to make questions.

1 you got an aspirin have ?
Have you got an aspirin?

2 a driving licence has got she ?

3 got you a cold have ?

4 they a nice house have got ?

5 we a new boss got have ?

6 Bill a brother got has ?

7 have you my keys got ?

8 Sonia a boyfriend got has ?

2 Make questions. Use the cues.

1 you / a newspaper?
Have you got a newspaper?

2 Sandra / a new flat?

3 you / an email address?

4 we / a new neighbour?

5 Fumiko / long hair?

6 they / a dog?

7 I / your new mobile number?

8 he / a laptop?

3 Choose the correct short answers.

1 Has he got a headache?
a No, he hasn't. ✓
b No, he haven't.

2 Have you got a new phone number?
a Yes, I has.
b Yes, I have.

3 Has she got a sister?
a Yes, she has.
b Yes, she is.

4 Have they got any children?
a No, they haven't.
b No, they haven't got.

5 Have we got a meeting today?
a No, we hasn't.
b No, we haven't.

6 Has Tim got a new car?
a Yes, he's got.
b Yes, he has.

7 Have I got an appointment this morning?
a Yes, you have.
b Yes, you got.

8 Has Fran got a good job?
a No, she hasn't got.
b No, she hasn't.

4 Answer these questions about yourself. Write more information about the things you have got.

1 Have you got a car?
No, I haven't. OR *Yes, I have. I've got a blue car.*

1 Have you got a car?

2 Have you got any brothers and sisters?

3 Have you got a job?

4 Have you got a good English teacher?

5 Have you got a private parking space?

6 Have you got a secretary?

7 Have you got any children?

8 Have you got your own office?

✓ Now ... *practise and learn.*

47 Common illnesses
Asking about people's health

1a Complete the words.

b Match the problems with the pictures.

1 I've got h_a_y fever. _e_
2 I've got a s___re throat. __
3 I've got a tem___erature. __
4 I've got st___mach ache. __
5 I've got a bad ba___k. __
6 I've got a cou___h. __
7 I've got a head___che. __
8 I've got too___hache. __

a

b
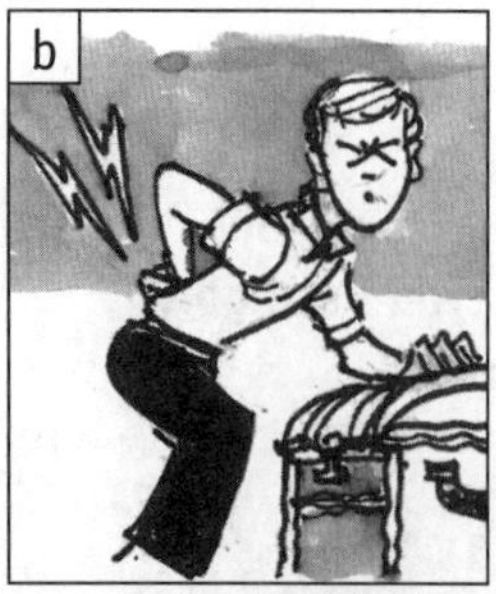
c

d

e

f

g

h

2a Complete the conversation. Use the words in the box.

cold dear ~~well~~ are matter

A Hello, Ken. How [1] _are_ you?
B Oh, I'm not very [2] ____________.
A Why? What's the [3] ____________?
B I've got a [4] ____________.
A Oh, [5] ____________.

✓ **Now ...** *practise and learn.*

b Write new conversations. Use the cues.

1 Sandra / a sore throat and a temperature

A Hello, Sandra. How ____________________?
B Oh, I'm ____________________.
A Why? ____________________?
B I've ____________________.
A ____________________.

2 Alan / a bad back

A ____________________
B ____________________
A ____________________
B ____________________
A ____________________

3 Complete the advice. Use the words in the box.

salt portions ~~smoke~~ exercise sun

1 Don't _smoke_ .

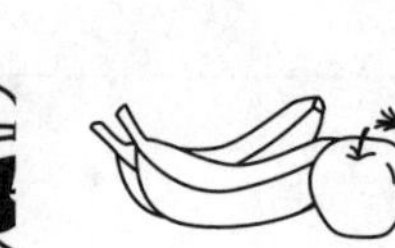

2 Do more ____________ .

3 Use less ____________ .

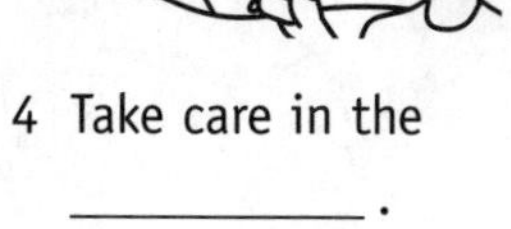

4 Take care in the ____________ .

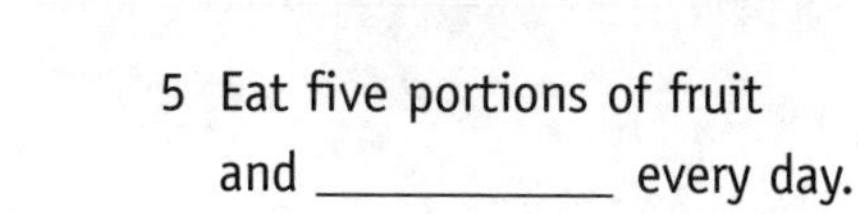

5 Eat five portions of fruit and ____________ every day.

48 Asking for things
Review: lessons 45–48

1 What's in Lydia's bag? Label the picture with the words in the box.

a piece of paper	a nail file	tissues	a towel	a stamp
scissors	~~plasters~~	a mirror	a pen	painkillers

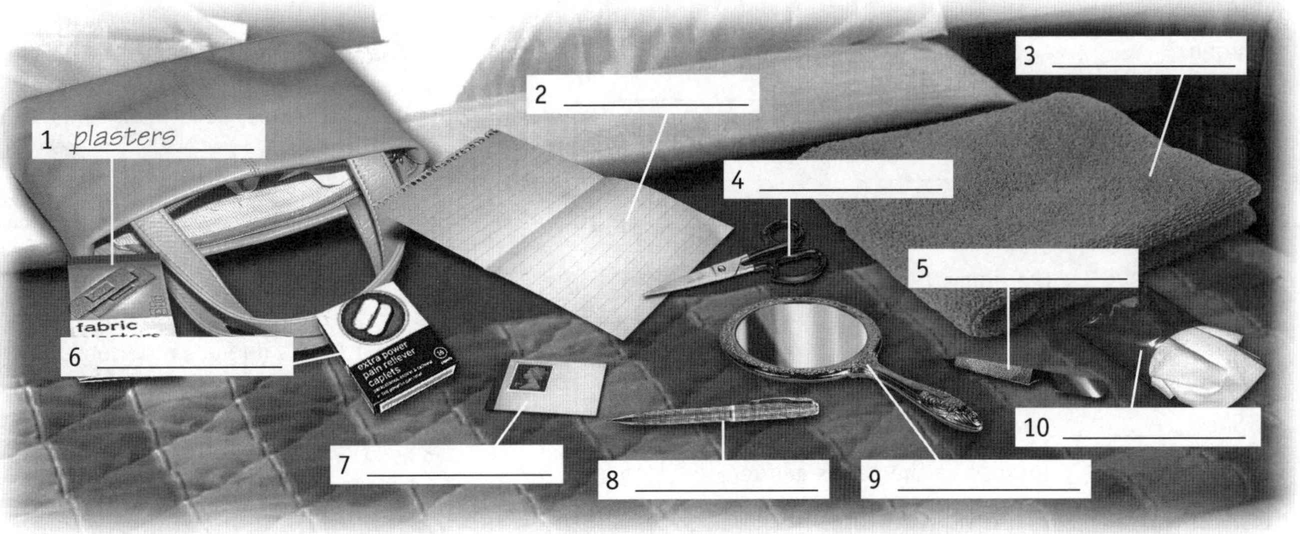

2a Choose the correct word.

1 I've got *some* / ~~*any*~~ tissues.
2 I haven't got *some* / *any* plasters.
3 Have you got *some* / *any* stamps?

b Complete with *some*, *any*, or *a*.

1 Have you got __a__ mirror?
2 I've got ______ stamps in my desk.
3 I'm sorry. I haven't got ______ painkillers.
4 I've got ______ pen in my bag.
5 Have you got ______ plasters?
6 I've got ______ tissues.

3 Complete the conversations. Use the words in the box.

have	you	haven't	~~got~~	please	here

1
A Have you ____got____ a piece of paper, please?
B Yes, I have. __________ you are.
A Thank __________.

2
A __________ you got __________ tissues, please?
B No, sorry. I __________.
A Oh, OK.

✓ **Now ...** ***practise and learn.***

Lessons 45–48

Choose the correct sentences.

1 a I've got the stomach ache.
 b I've got stomach ache.
2 a He hasn't got any money.
 b He haven't got any money.
3 a Have got you a girlfriend?
 b Have you got a girlfriend?
4 a I don't feel very well.
 b I'm not feel very well.
5 a What's the wrong?
 b What's the matter?
6 a I've got blue eyes.
 b I've got eyes blue.
7 a She hasn't got any tissues.
 b She doesn't have got any tissues.
8 a I've got some plasters.
 b I've got any plasters.

✓ **Now ...** ***review your progress.***

49 Activities
Writing: describing your leisure time

1 Complete the table. Use the activities in the box.

the guitar   football   the piano   ~~swimming~~   golf   skiing

go + verb + *-ing*	*play* + sports	*play* + *the* + musical instruments
running	basketball	the drums
swimming	________	________
cycling	ice hockey	the violin
________	________	________

2 Complete the sentences. Use the correct form of *go* or *play*.

1 He *plays* the drums.
2 They ________ skating on Mondays.
3 I ________ basketball.
4 She ________ swimming at the weekend.
5 We ________ football at the sports centre.
6 Jacek ________ the violin.
7 In my free time I ________ cycling.
8 Do you ________ skiing?
9 Does Jonas ________ ice hockey?
10 Carlos and Rita ________ running every day.

3 What do the people do in their free time? Complete the sentences. Use the correct form of the expressions in the box.

go swimming   paint   go skiing   play golf
go dancing   sing   ~~go skating~~   play the guitar

1 They *go skating* at the sports centre.

2 He ________ at the weekend.

3 We ________ on Saturdays.

4 He ________ in his free time.

5 He ________ every day.

6 She ________ in her free time.

7 I ________ on Sundays.

8 We ________ in the winter.

4 Answer the questions about yourself. When you answer *yes*, write extra information.

1 *Do you go swimming? No, I don't.* OR *Yes, I do. I go swimming on Fridays.*

1 Do you go swimming?
____
2 Do you cook?
____
3 Do you play a musical instrument?
____
4 What sports do you watch on TV?
____
5 Do you play any sports?
____
6 Do you go skiing?
____
7 Do you sing?
____
8 What do you do at the weekend?
____

✓ Now ... *practise and learn.*

50 *can / can't*
Writing: your abilities

1 Can the people do the activities? Make sentences with *can / can't* and the activities in the box.

swim cook play the violin sing ~~dance~~ play ice hockey

1 He *can't dance*.

2 I ________________.

3 They ________________.

4 He ________________.

5 She ________________.

6 I ________________.

2 Make questions and short answers about the pictures in exercise 1.

1 **A** *Can he dance?*
   B *No, he can't.*

2 **A** ________________
   B ________________

3 **A** ________________
   B ________________

4 **A** ________________
   B ________________

5 **A** ________________
   B ________________

6 **A** ________________
   B ________________

3a Match the parts of the expressions.

1 play the *h*	a marathon
2 eat with __	b yoga
3 ride a __	c cricket
4 run a __	d photographs
5 do __	e car
6 take good __	f bike
7 drive a __	g chopsticks
8 play __	h piano

b Can you do the activities in exercise 3a? Complete the sentences about yourself.

I can ________________________________
________________ and ________________.

I can't ________________________________
________________ or ________________.

4 Write about three more things that you can do, and three things that you can't do.

1 I can ________________.
2 I can ________________.
3 I can ________________.
4 I can't ________________.
5 I can't ________________.
6 I can't ________________.

51 Reading: a leisure survey
Writing: popular sports

1 Read the table. Complete the conversation.

Olivia		
Ability	***can/can't***	**Extra information**
speak foreign languages	✓	Japanese
swim	✗	
play sports	✓	volleyball, tennis
ride a horse	✓	
drive	✓	has got a new car
play a musical instrument	✓	the piano, the guitar
cook	✗	eats out a lot
use a computer	✓	

Interviewer So, Olivia. What things can you do? Can you speak any foreign languages?
Olivia [1] *Yes, I can*. I can speak [2] *Japanese*.
Interviewer Really? Very good. Now, can you swim?
Olivia [3] ____________.
Interviewer I see. Can you play any sports?
Olivia [4] ____________. I can [5] ____________.
Interviewer Can you ride a horse?
Olivia [6] ____________.
Interviewer And can you drive?
Olivia [7] ____________. I've got a new car.
Interviewer OK. And can you play a musical instrument?
Olivia [8] ____________. I can [9] ____________.
Interviewer I see. Can you cook?
Olivia [10] ____________. I eat out a lot.
Interviewer OK. And can you use a computer?
Olivia [11] ____________.
Interviewer OK. Thank you.

2 Answer the interviewer's questions about yourself. When you answer *yes*, write extra information.

1 Yes, I can. I can speak English (and …).
1 ____________
2 ____________
3 ____________
4 ____________
5 ____________
6 ____________
7 ____________
8 ____________

3 Are the sports popular in your country? Complete the table. Use the sports in the box.

American football	baseball	cricket
cycling	volleyball	golf
ice hockey	basketball	football
rugby	snooker	

Popular	Not popular

4 Complete the text about yourself.

My name's ____________ and I'm from ____________. ____________ and ____________ are (very) popular sports in my country, but ____________ isn't (very) popular. I can ____________ and ____________, but I can't ____________ or ____________.

✓ **Now …** ***practise and learn.***

52 Inviting someone to dinner
Review: lessons 49–52

1 Read the conversation. Are the statements below true (T) or false (F)?

Tim	Can I take you out to dinner?
Beth	Thank you. That would be nice.
Tim	We can try that new Italian restaurant.
Beth	*Bella Casa*?
Tim	Yes, that's right. Do you like Italian food?
Beth	Yes, I do. So, what day?
Tim	Is Friday OK for you?
Beth	No, sorry. I can't come on Friday.
Tim	Oh, well, what about Thursday, then?
Beth	Yes, Thursday's fine. Is eight o'clock OK for you?
Tim	Fine. See you at the restaurant at eight on Thursday.
Beth	OK.

1 _F_ Beth wants to take Tim to dinner.
2 ___ They want to go to a Chinese restaurant.
3 ___ The restaurant's name is *Bella Casa*.
4 ___ Beth can't come on Friday.
5 ___ Their date is on Wednesday.
6 ___ It's at 7.30.

2 Match the halves of the expressions.

1 Can I _e_	a OK for you?
2 That would ___	b come on Tuesday.
3 Is Tuesday ___	c Thursday?
4 Sorry. I can't ___	d be nice.
5 What about ___	e take you out to lunch?

3a Complete the conversation. Use the expressions in exercise 2 to help you.

A [1] _Can I take_ you out to lunch?
B Yes. That [2] ________________.
A [3] ________________ for you?
B No, sorry. [4] ________________ on Tuesday.
A Well, [5] ________________ Thursday?
B Yes. Thursday's fine.

b Make a new conversation. Use the cues.

dinner / Friday / Saturday
A Can I take you ________________?
B Yes, __________ would ________________.
A Is Friday ________________?
B No, __________. I can't ________________.
A Well, __________ about ________________?
B Yes, ________________.

✓ **Now ...** ***practise and learn.***

Lessons 49–52

Choose the correct sentences.

1 a I can to swim.
  b I can swim.
2 a She can't ski.
  b She can't skiing.
3 a Would you like go to the cinema?
  b Would you like to go to the cinema?
4 a We can't play cricket.
  b We don't can play cricket.
5 a Can fix you a computer?
  b Can you fix a computer?
6 a Peter can plays the violin.
  b Peter can play the violin.
7 a Can you ride a horse?
  b Do you can ride a horse?
8 a We go cycle on Saturdays.
  b We go cycling on Saturdays.

✓ **Now ...** ***review your progress.***

53 Parts of a house

1 Label the picture. Use the words in the box.

the dining room	the garage	the living room	upstairs
a window	the stairs	the cellar	the bathroom
~~a bedroom~~	the balcony	the garden	the hall
the kitchen	a door	downstairs	

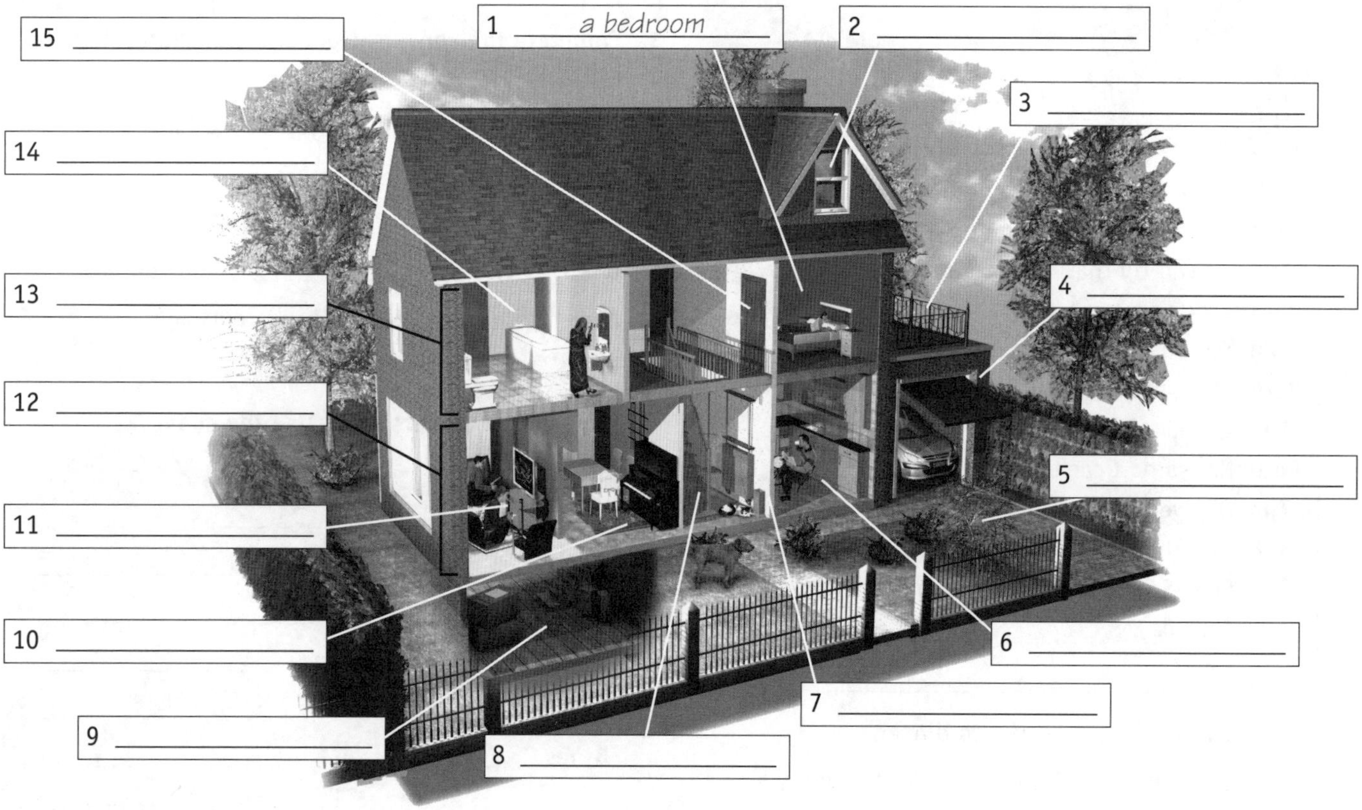

2 Write the names of the parts of a house.

1 You eat here.
the d i n i n g room
2 You cook here.
the ______________
3 You watch TV here.
the ____________ room
4 You sleep here.
a ______________
5 You have a shower here.
the ______________
6 This is under the house.
the ____________

3 Answer the questions about your home.

1 Where is the telephone?
It's in the ...
2 Do you put your car in a garage?
____
3 Is your bedroom upstairs?
____
4 Where do you eat breakfast?
____
5 Where is the television?
____
6 Where do you do your homework?
____

54 Describing your home

1 Look at the picture. Complete the sentences. Use *There's, There are, There isn't,* or *There aren't.*

1 ___There's___ a desk next to the window.
2 ______________ three boxes next to the desk.
3 ______________ a computer on the desk.
4 ______________ a telephone on the desk.
5 ______________ any books on the desk.
6 ______________ some keys in front of the computer.
7 ______________ a bed in the room.
8 ______________ any people in the room.

2 Choose the correct sentences.

1 a There's a telephone in the hall. ✓
  b There are a telephone in the hall.

2 a How many flats there are in your block?
  b How many flats are there in your block?

3 Is there a balcony?
  a Yes, there has.
  b Yes, there is.

4 a There's two people in the house.
  b There are two people in the house.

5 a Is there a kitchen?
  b Is a kitchen there?

6 a There has a TV in the living room.
  b There is a TV in the living room.

3 Marta wants a new home. Igor has got a flat. Complete their phone conversation. Use *there is, there's, there are, there isn't, there aren't, is there,* or *are there.*

Marta Can I ask some questions about the flat? 1___Is there___ a good view?

Igor Yes, 2___there is___. You can see the park.

Marta That's nice. And how many bedrooms 3______________?

Igor 4______________ five. You share with four students.

Marta That's fine. I'm a student, too. 5______________ any TVs in the flat?

Igor Yes, 6______________ two. 7______________ a big TV in the living room, and a small one in the kitchen.

Marta 8______________ two bathrooms?

Igor No, 9______________. 10______________ just one bathroom.

Marta 11______________ a desk in the room?

Igor No, 12______________. There's a bed, and two chairs, but no desk.

Marta That's OK. Can I see the room, please?

Igor Yes. How about Friday at eight o'clock?

Marta Great.

4 Answer the questions about your house or flat.

1 How many people are there in your house or flat?
*There are ...*______________

2 How many rooms are there?
____

3 Is there a garden?
____

4 Is there a cellar?
____

5 How many bedrooms are there?
____

6 Is there a TV in your bedroom?
____

55 Reading and writing: describing homes
Pronunciation: *th* sounds

1 Read the conversation. Choose the correct answers.

1 Who has got a new flat?	Max	Scott
2 Does he live there alone?	Yes	No
3 Does he like it?	Yes	No

Max Do you like your new flat, Scott?
Scott Yes, it's great. It's in one of those modern blocks near the sports centre.
Max Oh, right. How many rooms are there?
Scott Well, there are four bedrooms. Then there's a kitchen and a living room and a hall. There's a dining room, too, but we don't eat there. We use it as an office. We eat in the living room. Oh, and there are two bathrooms, too.
Max That's good. How many flats are there in the block?
Scott Ten, I think. We're on the top floor.
Max Is there a good view?
Scott Yes, there is. There's a big balcony and we sit there in the evening. We love it.
Max Is there a lift?
Scott Yes, there is, fortunately. There are five floors and that's a lot of stairs! Anyway, come and visit us at the weekend.
Max OK. That would be nice. Thanks.

2 Read the conversation again. Choose the correct words and phrases.

1 The flat is in *a modern* / ~~*an old*~~ block.
2 It's near the *supermarket* / *sports centre*.
3 There are *two* / *four* bedrooms.
4 They eat in the *kitchen* / *living room*.
5 They use the dining room as *a bedroom* / *an office*.
6 There are two *bathrooms* / *garages*.
7 There are *ten* / *twelve* flats in the block.
8 The flat is on the *first* / *top* floor.
9 *There's* / *There isn't* a lift.
10 They sit *in the garden* / *on the balcony* in the evening.

3 Read the email. Change the bold words and phrases to make it true for you.

My home is a **flat**. It's in **the city centre**, near **a hospital and a shopping centre**. There are **five** people at home – **my parents, my two brothers**, and me. There are **eight** rooms in the **flat**: **a kitchen**, **a living room**, **two bathrooms** and **four bedrooms**. **The kitchen** is my favourite room. **We cook** and **eat** there, and **we listen to the radio**. There's a **large balcony**, and a **garage in a block**, but there isn't a **garden** or a **cellar**.

My home is a …

____
____
____
____
____
____
____
____

✓ **Now …** ***practise and learn.***

4 Pronunciation Are the *th* sounds voiced or unvoiced? Complete the table. Use the words in the box.

~~bathroom~~ ~~there~~ Thursday thing these thirteen with mother thanks that

Voiced *th* sound /ð/	Unvoiced *th* sound /θ/
bathroom	*there*

56 Ordinal numbers; asking and saying where things are
Review: lessons 53–56

1 Complete the numbers of the floors.

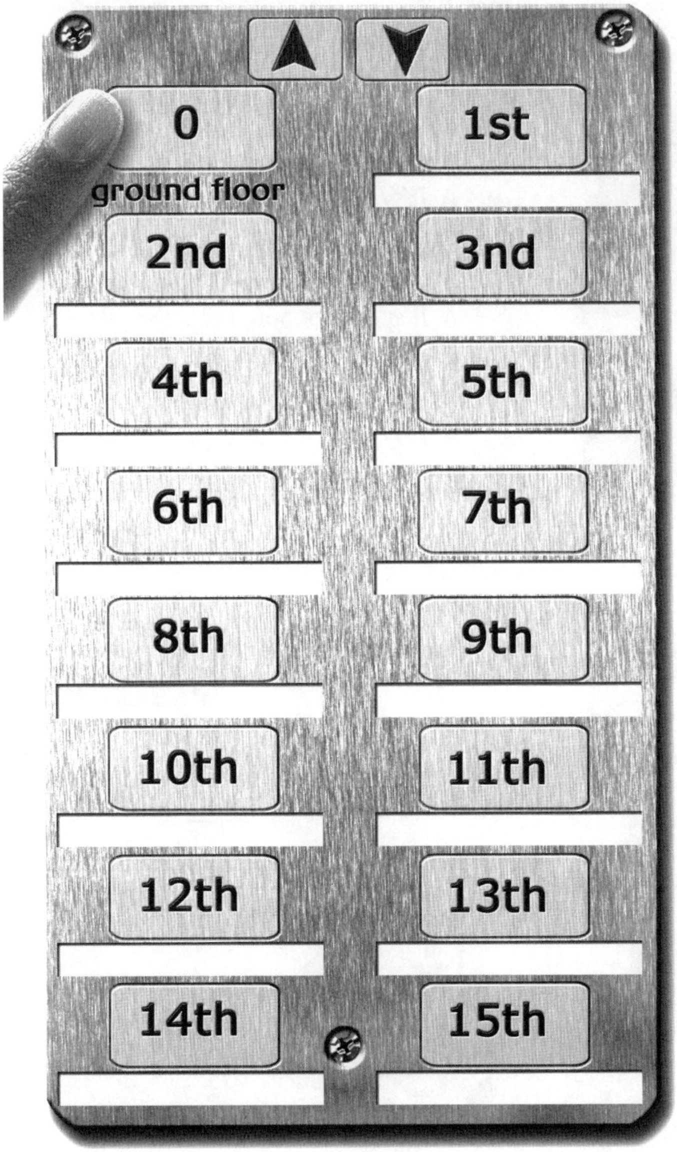

2 Match the descriptions with the doors.

1 __29__ It's the third door on the left.
2 ______ The kitchen is the second door on the right.
3 ______ The meeting's in the first room on the right.
4 ______ My room is the first door on the left.
5 ______ His office is the second room on the left.
6 ______ That's the third door on the right.

3 Choose the correct words.

1 **A** Excuse me. Where *can* / ~~*do*~~ I find Room 52, please?
B It's on the *four* / *fourth* floor.
A Thank you.

2 **A** Excuse me. Is *there* / *where* a cash machine near here, please?
B Yes, there's a cash machine *on* / *of* London Road. That's the third *floor* / *street* on the left.
A Thank you.

3 **A** Excuse me. Where *there* / *is* the bathroom, please?
B It's *over* / *near* there – the first *floor* / *door* on the right.
A Thank you.

Lessons 53–56

Choose the correct sentences.

1 a How many students there are in your class?
b How many students are there in your class?
2 a The restaurant's on the fifth floor.
b The restaurant's on the five floor.
3 a There no is a lift in this block.
b There isn't a lift in this block.
4 a The restaurant is in Market Street.
b The restaurant is at Market Street.
5 a There's four rooms upstairs.
b There are four rooms upstairs.
6 a Is there a good view? Yes, there is.
b Has it got a good view? Yes, there is.
7 a My room's on third floor.
b My room's on the third floor.
8 a Excuse me, is a bank near here?
b Excuse me, is there a bank near here?

✓ **Now ...** ***review your progress.***

57 Clothes

1 Match the pictures with the clothes.

_10_ a top	___ socks	___ a shirt	___ jeans
___ a suit	___ trousers	___ a skirt	___ shoes
___ a jacket	___ a jumper	___ boots	___ shorts
___ a tie	___ a T-shirt	___ trainers	___ a dress

2 Complete the table. Use the words in the box.

~~jumper~~ ~~clothes~~ jacket shorts T-shirt shoes dress jeans

Singular	How much is Do you like	this that	skirt, shirt, _jumper_ ___, ___, ___?
Plural	How much are Do you like	these those	trousers, _clothes_ ___, ___, ___?

3a Choose the correct words and phrases.

1 **A** Do you like ~~this~~ / *these* trousers?
B Yes, I do. How much *is it* / *are they*?
A *It's* / *They're* £42.

2 **A** Do you like *this* / *these* dress?
B Yes, I do. How much *is it* / *are they*?
A *It's* / *hey're* €84.

3 **A** Do you like *this* / *these* jeans?
B Yes, I do. How much *is it* / *are they*?
A *It's* / *They're* $60.

4 **A** Do you like *this* / *these* jacket?
B Yes, I do. How much *is it* / *are they*?
A *It's* / *They're* €100.

b Write conversations for the items below.

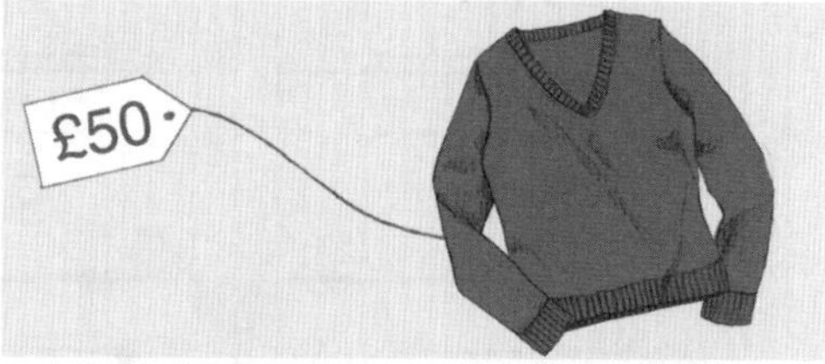

A Do you like ___________________?
B Yes, I do. How ___________________?
A ___________________.

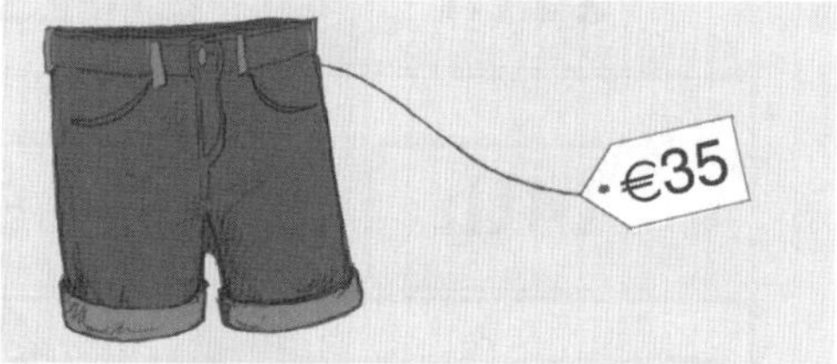

A Do you like ___________________?
B Yes, I do. How ___________________?
A ___________________.

4 Write about your clothes today.

a green shirt, black trousers, a ...

____

____

____

____

____

____

58 Present continuous: *statements*
Spelling of *-ing* forms

1 Complete the sentences. Use short forms of *be*: *'m*, *'s*, or *'re*.

1 She *'s* swimming.
2 I___ eating a sandwich.
3 We___ having lunch.
4 They___ going to work.
5 He___ using the Internet.
6 You___ sitting in my seat!
7 Lucy___ driving to work.
8 I___ writing a letter.

2 Complete the table.

Spelling of *-ing* forms		
+ *-ing*	**Remove *-e* + *-ing***	**Double consonant + *-ing***
go *going*	ride *riding*	run *running*
play ______	have ______	sit ______
eat ______	write ______	get ______
read ______	make ______	swim ______
clean ______	drive ______	
send ______		
wear ______		

3 What are the people doing? Use the activities in the box.

get up	take a photograph	run
watch TV	~~drive a sports car~~	play tennis

1 He *'s driving a sports car*.

2 They ______________.

3 She ______________.

4 We______________.

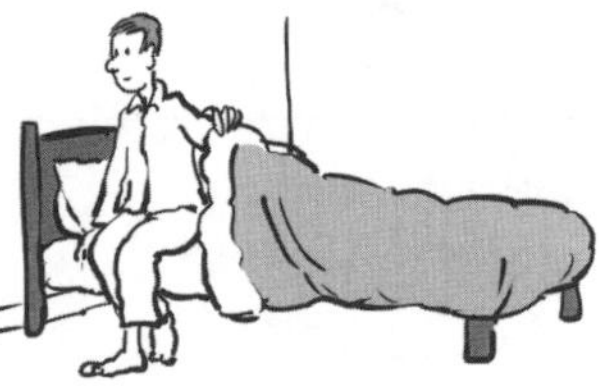

5 He ______________.

6 They ______________.

4 Make the sentences negative.

1 I'm reading a newspaper.
I'm not reading a newspaper.

2 We're going to the supermarket.
____

3 They're playing golf.
____

4 He's wearing trainers.
____

5 She's having a shower.
____

6 I'm using the computer.
____

7 You're eating my sandwich.
____

8 It's raining.
____

5 Are you doing these things at the moment? Make sentences.

1 *I'm wearing jeans.* OR
I'm not wearing jeans.

1 wear jeans
____

2 drive a car
____

3 sit at a desk
____

4 write
____

5 swim
____

6 listen to music
____

7 watch TV
____

8 play tennis
____

59 Reading and writing: describing people

1 Read the conversation. Label the people. Use the names in the box.

Juanita Michael Tricia Meena Elke Sanjit

A Meena's at that table over there. She's wearing a dress and boots, and she's drinking a cup of coffee. Her husband Sanjit is there, too. He's wearing a suit, and he's reading a newspaper.

B Who's the other man? He's sitting at the table on the right. He's reading a book.

A That's Michael. He's having lunch.

B Oh, OK, and who are the women at the table on the left?

A They're Juanita and Elke. They're looking at some photographs, and they're talking. They're having a drink, too, but they aren't eating. Elke is wearing jeans, and Juanita's wearing a lovely skirt.

B I see. Who's that woman over there? She's standing near Meena, and she's talking on her mobile phone.

A That's Tricia.

2a Are the statements true (T) or false (F)?

1 _F_ Tricia is drinking a cup of coffee.
2 __ Juanita and Elke are standing up.
3 __ Michael is sitting with Meena.
4 __ Tricia is talking to Elke.
5 __ Michael isn't wearing a suit.
6 __ Elke is reading a book.
7 __ Juanita is wearing a skirt.
8 __ Meena and Sanjit are eating.

b Correct the false sentences.

1 *Tricia isn't drinking a cup of coffee.*

____

____

____

____

____

____

____

3 Complete the labels.

60 Saying goodbye
Review: lessons 57–60

1 Underline the eight mistakes in the summary of the story.

Ryan gives Jordan a ticket for the football match. Jordan rings Lucy, but she is talking on her phone. Ryan leaves the coffee shop. Cindy is unhappy because her sister is coming. Lucy is leaving her flat. Her friends are going to the cinema, but she isn't going with them. She is going on a date with Ryan. At nine o'clock, Lucy is sitting alone at home. Ryan and Jordan are watching a rock concert. Peter sees them on TV.

2 Put the words in the correct order to make sentences.

1 tomorrow you see

See you tomorrow.

2 nice a have time

____

3 you later see

____

4 won't be I long

____

3 Complete the conversations. Use the expressions in exercise 2.

1

Man I'm going to the bank. *See* *you* *later*.

Woman But we've got a meeting at 3 o'clock.

Man It's OK. I ________ ________ ________.

2

Woman Bye. I'm going to the cinema now.

Man H________ ________ ________ ________.

Woman Thanks. S________ ________ t________.

Lessons 57–60

Choose the correct sentences.

1 a Do you like these jeans?
  b Do you like this jeans?

2 a She isn't go to work.
  b She isn't going to work.

3 a We're shoping.
  b We're shopping.

4 a I'm wearing a blue suit.
  b I wearing a blue suit.

5 a They are swimming.
  b They is swimming.

6 a We aren't watching TV.
  b We no watching TV.

7 a I'm driveing a van.
  b I'm driving a van.

8 a She's don't talking on her mobile.
  b She isn't talking on her mobile.

✓ **Now ...** ***review your progress.***

61 Transport
Pronunciation: vowel sounds /æ/ and /ɑː/

1a Complete the grid. Use forms of transport.

T	R	A	1 M			
		C	2		C	H
			3	A	X	
		B	4		T	
	C	A	5			
			6	U		
T	R		7	N		
	B		8	E		
		F	9		R	Y

b Find the hidden word.

The hidden word is

1 M 2___ 3___ 4___ 5___ 6___ 7___ 8___ 9___ .

2 Solve the anagrams and write the words.

1 a sbu ptos

a bus stop

2 het derdnounugr

____

3 a taniots

____

4 na trirapo

____

5 a sub notatis

____

6 a xtia nark

____

3 Match the descriptions with the places.

1 You go here to take the train. c
2 You can see a lot of buses here. ___
3 You wait for a taxi here. ___
4 You take the plane here. ___
5 You wait for a bus here. ___

a an airport
b a bus stop
c a train station
d a taxi rank
e a bus station

4 Choose the correct sentences.

1 a She's going with train.
  b She's going by train. ✓
2 a He's going to the party by the motorbike.
  b He's going to the party by motorbike.
3 a They're waiting for the bus.
  b They're waiting the bus.
4 a I'm travelling for the underground.
  b I'm travelling by the underground
5 a Why don't you go by taxi?
  b Why don't you go in taxi?
6 a We're going by boat.
  b We're getting by boat.
7 a I'm waiting for train.
  b I'm waiting for the train.

5 Pronunciation Tick (✓) the pairs of words with the same vowel sounds.

1	**trav**el	**sta**tion
2	plane	train ✓
3	**tax**i	bag
4	take	wait
5	late	flat
6	bank	make
7	place	have
8	play	table

62 Present continuous: questions

1 Make questions.

1 They're waiting for the bus.

Are they waiting for the bus?

2 She's having lunch.

__________ lunch?

3 You're having a good time.

__________ a good time?

4 I'm sitting in your seat.

__________ in your seat?

5 We're taking the underground.

__________ the underground?

6 You're watching the news.

__________ the news?

7 The computer's working now.

__________ now?

8 The trains are running late.

__________ late?

2 Match the questions with the short answers.

1 Are you having a good time? *b*

2 Is Raj fixing a computer? __

3 Are we waiting for the number 27 bus? __

4 Am I looking at the right page? __

5 Is Tania playing volleyball? __

6 Are you reading the newspaper? __

7 Is your mobile working now? __

a No, I'm not. You can have it.
b Yes, I am.
c Yes, it is. Thanks.
d No, he isn't.
e Yes, she is.
f No, we aren't. We're waiting for the number 30.
g No, you aren't. It's on page 24.

3 Complete the questions. Use the cues.

1 **A** What *are you eating*? (you / eat)
B It's a cheese sandwich.

2 **A** Where __________? (they / go)
B To the station.

3 **A** What __________? (she / wear)
B A blue dress.

4 **A** What __________? (they / do)
B They're sitting on the beach.

5 **A** Who __________ for? (you / wait)
B My boyfriend. He's late – as usual.

6 **A** What __________? (you / watch)
B It's an Indian film.

4 Choose the correct sentences.

1 a Where are you going? ✓
b Where you are going?

2 Are they taking the train?
a Yes, they're taking.
b Yes, they are.

3 Is she having a shower?
a Yes, she's.
b Yes, she is.

4 a Are they sitting on the beach?
b Sitting are they on the beach?

5 a What you do?
b What are you doing?

6 a You watching TV?
b Are you watching TV?

5 What are you doing at the moment? Answer the questions about yourself.

1 Yes, I am. OR *No, I'm not.*

1 Are you sitting at a desk?

____

2 Are you using a computer?

____

3 Are you wearing jeans?

____

4 Are you talking?

____

5 Are you listening to music?

____

6 Are you eating?

____

7 Are you working at home?

____

8 Are you having a good time?

____

63 Reading and writing: postcards

1 Complete the sentences. Use *in* or *on*.

1 He's _on_ the bus.
2 I'm ______ a taxi.
3 My bag's ______ the car.
4 Is she ______ holiday?
5 They're ______ a boat.
6 Is he here ______ business?
7 I'm ______ the train.
8 He's ______ Brazil.
9 We're ______ Tokyo.
10 Are you ______ the beach?

2a Match the pictures with the postcards.

b Complete the postcards. Use the *-ing* form of the verbs in the boxes.

A ☐

B ☐

1 have ~~sit~~ write swim look after

Hello from Australia. I'm on holiday in Sydney with Ellie and John. At the moment I'm [1] _sitting_ on Bondai Beach. Ellie and John are [2] ______________ in the sea. I'm [3] ______________ our bags and wallets, and I'm [4] ______________ some postcards. We're [5] ______________ a great time. Sydney's a beautiful city.
Hope you're OK.
love, Paula

2 enjoy take do travel

Dear Uma,
I'm in France on business. I'm [1] ______________ from Paris to Marseilles with Pierre and Amélie from our French office. We're [2] ______________ the TGV train. It's very fast! At the moment, Amelie and Pierre are [3] ______________ some work on their laptops. I'm really [4] ______________ the trip, and the food is fantastic.
See you soon.
Ken

3 Read the completed postcards. Choose the correct answers.

1 Where is Paula?
  a on the beach ✓
  b on a train

2 Where is Ken going?
  a to Paris
  b to Marseilles

3 What are Ellie and John doing?
  a They're playing volleyball on the beach.
  b They're swimming.

4 What is Amélie doing?
  a She's working on her laptop.
  b She's reading a magazine.

5 How is Ken travelling?
  a by car
  b by train

6 Are Paula, Ellie and John enjoying their holiday?
  a Yes, they are.
  b No, they aren't.

4 Write your own postcard. Use the postcards in exercise 2 to help you.

Dear ______________,
I'm on ______________________
in ______________________ with
______________________.
At the moment I'm ______________
____
and ______________________
are ______________________.
We're ______________________
a great time. ______________ is
______________________.
Hope ______________________
______________,
____

✓ Now ... *practise and learn.*

64 Talking about plans
Review: lessons 61–64

1 What's Emilio doing next week? Read his diary. Complete the sentences.

M	*10a.m. go to the dentist's*
T	*2p.m. meet visitors from Cairo*
W	*p.m. take the visitors to the airport*
Th	*afternoon play basketball*
Fr	*evening go to Bruno's party*
S	*look after the children*
S	*have lunch with Elena's parents*

1 On Monday morning *he's going to the dentist's*.
2 On Tuesday afternoon he's ______________________ from Cairo.
3 On Wednesday afternoon he ______________________.
4 On Thursday afternoon ______________________.
5 On Friday evening ______________________.
6 On Saturday ______________________.
7 On Sunday ______________________.

2 Describe your week next week.

1 On Monday morning I'm *going to the doctor's* ______________________.
2 On Tuesday afternoon ______________________.
3 On Wednesday afternoon ______________________.
4 On Thursday evening ______________________.
5 On Friday evening ______________________.
6 On Saturday ______________________.
7 On Sunday ______________________.

✓ **Now …** ***practise and learn.***

3 Match the parts of the signs.

1 **minimum** *c*
2 **waiting** ___
3 **Terminal** ___
4 **Fasten** ___
5 **Please queue** ___

a **one: international arrivals**
b **your seatbelt**
c **charge £5**
d **this side**
e **room**

Lessons 61–64

Choose the correct sentences.

1 a Are taking they the ferry?
  b Are they taking the ferry?
2 a What you are watching?
  b What are you watching?
3 a We're waiting for the bus.
  b We're waiting the bus.
4 a I'm taking the train.
  b I'm taking train.
5 a We're on the plane.
  b We're in the plane.
6 a Are you travelling with boat?
  b Are you travelling by boat?
7 a 'Are they going on holiday?' 'Yes, they're.'
  b 'Are they going on holiday?' 'Yes, they are.'
8 a 'Are you having a good time?' 'Yes, I'm having.'
  b 'Are you having a good time?' 'Yes, I am.'

✓ **Now …** ***review your progress.***

65 Saying where people are
Prepositions of place

1 Complete the table. Use the words in the box.

~~a meeting~~	~~home~~	bed	a party	the doctor's
the garden	the shower	work	the supermarket	a restaurant

He can't come to the phone. He's	**in**	*a meeting* . ________ . ________ . ________ .
She isn't here. She's	**at**	*home* . ________ . ________ . ________ . ________ . ________ .

2 Where are the people? Complete the sentences.

1 They're *in a meeting* .

2 She's ________ .

3 He's ________ .

4 They're ________ .

5 They're ________ .

6 She's ________ .

7 They're ________ .

8 He's ________ .

3 Choose the correct words and phrases.

1 **A** Hello. Can I speak to Doctor Carter, please?
B I'm sorry. He's ~~*here*~~ / *on holiday* this week.

2 **A** Hello. Can I speak to Mrs Bell, please?
B I'm sorry. She isn't *here / away* this week.

3 **A** Hello. Is Dev *in / out*?
B Yes, he is. Just a minute.

4 **A** Hello. Can I speak to Mr Ferreira, please?
B I'm sorry. He's *in / out* at the moment.

5 **A** Hello. Can I speak to Alicia, please?
B I'm sorry. She's *on holiday / away* today. She's ill.

4 Think of five people that you know. Where are they now?

My son is at school.

1 ________

2 ________

3 ________

4 ________

5 ________

66 Past simple: *to be*, statements
Pronunciation: syllables in negative verb forms

1 Complete the sentences. Use *was* or *were*.

1 We [1] ___were___ at a party on Saturday night. It [2]________ at our neighbours' house. It [3]________ a good party. All our friends [4]________ there. We [5]________ there till three o'clock in the morning.

2 Jack [1]________ away last week. He [2]________ on holiday with his family. They [3]________ in Tenerife.

3 I [1]________ in Berlin yesterday. I [2]________ at a conference. A lot of people [3]________ there. The people from our German office [4]________ there, too.

2 Make the sentences negative.

1 I was at home last night.
___I wasn't___ at home last night.

2 They were at school yesterday.
__________________ at school yesterday.

3 He was ill on Tuesday.
__________________ ill on Tuesday.

4 We were on holiday last week.
__________________ on holiday last week.

5 Ela was on holiday last week.
__________________ on holiday last week.

6 You were at our party.
__________________ at our party.

3 Complete the table. Use the expressions in the box.

today ~~last week~~ yesterday
tonight yesterday evening

the past	the present
last week	this week
________	________
last night	________
________	this evening

4 Make sentences. Use the cues.

1 in (✗) at the sports centre (✓)
I ___wasn't in___ last night.
I ___was at the sports centre___.

2 at work (✓) ill (✗)
She __________________ yesterday.
She __________________.

3 in the shower (✓) in bed (✗)
I __________________.
I __________________.

4 at home (✗) at the cinema (✓)
We __________________ last night.
We __________________.

5 very good (✓) expensive (✗)
The hotel __________________.
It __________________.

5 Complete the sentences about yourself.

1 I was ___at work___ yesterday.
2 I wasn't ________________ at the weekend.
3 I was ________________ yesterday evening.
4 I wasn't ________________ last week.
5 I was ________________ last night.
6 I wasn't ________________ on Saturday evening.

✓ Now … *practise and learn.*

6 Pronunciation How many syllables? Complete the table. Use the negative forms in the box.

~~isn't~~ ~~don't~~ wasn't doesn't weren't
aren't haven't can't hasn't

one syllable	two syllables
don't	*isn't*
________	________
________	________
________	________
	________

67 Past simple: *to be*, questions

1 Make questions.

1 You were out yesterday afternoon.

Were you out yesterday afternoon?

2 They were on holiday last week.

______

3 Mohammed was at a football match on Friday.

______

4 The film was good.

______

5 Sunita was at the dentist's on Tuesday morning.

______

6 We were at the supermarket last Wednesday.

______

7 He was late on Monday.

______

8 You were at the meeting.

______

2a Make questions. Use the cues.

b Complete the short answers.

1 Mick and Rosie / away last week?

A *Were Mick and Rosie away last week?*

B Yes, *they were*.

2 they / on holiday?

A ______

B Yes, ______.

3 they / in Turkey?

A ______

B No, ______.

4 Rosie / ill?

A ______

B Yes, ______.

5 she / in bed for two days

A ______

B No, ______.

3 Answer the questions about yourself.

1 Were you at home yesterday evening?

Yes, I was. OR *No, I wasn't.*

2 Were you ill last week?

______

3 Were you at work / school yesterday?

______

4 Where were you at six o'clock this morning?

I was ______

5 Where were you on Saturday afternoon?

I was ______

6 Where were you on your birthday?

I was ______

4 What is American, and what is British? Write *the UK* or *the USA*.

1 I'm going to the **store**. *the USA*

2 I live in a **flat**. ______

3 The **lift** is over there. ______

4 We don't play **soccer** here. ______

5 They're on **vacation**. ______

68 Expressing anger
Review: lessons 65–68

1 Number the sentences in the correct order to tell the story.

a ___ Lucy is angry with Jordan, because he wasn't at the restaurant.

b _6_ Cindy is very angry with Ryan now.

c _1_ It's the day after the football match. Lucy and Jordan are at The Coffee Shop.

d ___ Cindy asks about the football match. Peter says Ryan was there.

e ___ Ryan takes the dog for a walk.

f ___ Lucy is very angry with Jordan. She leaves The Coffee Shop.

g ___ Peter comes into The Coffee Shop. He says Jordan was at the football match.

2a Complete the expressions.

1 I'm very angry w_______ you.

2 That's i___!

3 Don't t_______ to me!

4 It was v_______ embarrassing.

b Who says the expressions?

a Cindy
b Lucy
c Peter

3 Complete the sentences about the story. Use *was, wasn't, were,* or *weren't*.

1 On Wednesday night Lucy ___was___ at a restaurant for an hour.
2 She __________ alone.
3 Her friends __________ at the restaurant.
4 They __________ at a rock concert.
5 Jordan __________ at the restaurant with Lucy.
6 He __________ with Ryan.
7 They __________ at a football match.
8 Peter __________ at the match.
9 The match __________ on TV.
10 Ryan and Jordan __________ in the crowd.

Lessons 65–68

Choose the correct sentences.

1 a She wasn't at work on Monday.
  b She wasn't at the work on Monday.
2 a Where were you yesterday?
  b Where you were yesterday?
3 a He's at bed.
  b He's in bed.
4 a We was out last night.
  b We were out last night.
5 a Do you were away last week?
  b Were you away last week?
6 a I was in shower.
  b I was in the shower.
7 a She was at the cinema.
  b She were at the cinema.
8 a He no was at home yesterday.
  b He wasn't at home yesterday.

✓ Now ... *review your progress.*

69 Emergency services
Reading and writing: emergency services

1 Complete the table. Use the words in the box.

officer fire brigade police station ambulance police paramedic fire station fire engine ~~hospital~~

Emergency service	People	Vehicles	Places	Things
Medical services	a ______	an ______	a *hospital* ______	a first aid kit
The ______	a fire fighter	a ______	a ______	a fire alarm
The ______	a police ______	a police car	a ______	

2 Match the sentences with the pictures.

1 I'm a police officer. I work at a police station. *c*

2 Oh no! There's a fire in the kitchen. Dial 999 and call the fire brigade! __

3 Stop. Thief! Quick! Call the police! __

4 I work at a fire station. When we hear the fire alarm, we run to the fire engines. __

a

b

c

d

3a Read the text about emergency services in Hungary. Are the statements true (T) or false (F)?

1 *F* The police wear blue uniforms.

2 __ Police cars are blue, and have white lights.

3 __ You can call a different number for ambulances and the fire brigade.

4 __ The uniforms of paramedics are green.

5 __ You can call 112 or 107 for the police.

6 __ Fire engines and fire alarms are different colours.

b Replace the words in bold and rewrite the text to make it true for your country.

In **Hungary**, you call **112** for the emergency services. **You can call different numbers for each service – 107 for the police, 104 for an ambulance, or 105 for the fire brigade**. The police wear **grey** uniforms, and they drive **white** cars with **blue lights**. Ambulances are **usually white and red** and **paramedics** wear **white or black** uniforms. Fire alarms and fire engines are **red**.

____

____

____

____

____

____

____

____

____

____

✓ **Now ...** *practise and learn.*

70 Past simple: regular verbs
Pronunciation: syllables in *-ed* endings

1a Choose the correct verbs.

Last week I [1]*decided/ ~~played~~* to have a short holiday in Spain.
On Thursday I [2]*started/ finished* work at 12 o'clock and I [3]*called/ cleaned* a taxi to go to the airport.

At half past two I was at the airport, when the fire alarm [4]*stopped/ sounded*. Everyone [5]*used/ picked* up their bags and [6]*rushed/ cycled* outside.

b Continue the story. Put the verbs into the past simple.

The fire brigade and the police [1] *arrived* (arrive) and they [2]____________ (close) the airport. We [3]____________ (wait) in the car park. It was cold, and then it [4]____________ (start) to rain. Finally, they [5]____________ (open) the airport again and I [6]____________ (travel) to Madrid.

c Finish the story. Use the verbs in the box in the past simple.

need rain watch stay travel ~~arrive~~

When I [1] *arrived* in Madrid, I was ill.
I [2]____________ in bed in the hotel for two days and I [3]____________ TV. On Sunday I was OK, but it [4]____________ all day. On Sunday evening I [5]____________ back to London. After that I [6]____________ a holiday.

2 Write sentences about your life last week. Use the cues.

1 *I watched a good football match on Wednesday.*

1 ______________________________ (watch)
2 ______________________________ (listen to)
3 ______________________________ (play)
4 ______________________________ (travel)
5 ______________________________ (phone)
6 ______________________________ (walk)

✓ Now ... *practise and learn.*

3a Pronunciation How many syllables? Write the number in the brackets.

	Present simple	Past simple	Extra syllable?
1	stop (1)	stopped (*1*)	
2	start (1)	started (*2*)	✓
3	watch (1)	watched (___)	
4	use (1)	used (___)	
5	need (1)	needed (___)	
6	wait (1)	waited (___)	
7	arrive (2)	arrived (___)	
8	decide (2)	decided (___)	
9	walk (1)	walked (___)	
10	want (1)	wanted (___)	

b Tick (✓) the verbs with an extra syllable in the past simple.

71 Reading: a story in the past
Writing: connecting ideas with *because*

1 Read the story and answer the questions below.

It was Jill Mason's fiftieth birthday last Thursday. Her friend, Faith, invited her for lunch at a local Italian restaurant. They really enjoyed the lunch and they talked for a long time about their days at school together.

At half past three, Jill called a taxi. When she arrived home, she opened the front door, but then she stopped in the hall. There were voices in the living room. But who was it? Her husband, Harry, was at work and their son, Peter, was away at university. Jill listened. There were two or three people in the living room.

She walked out of the house again and phoned the police on her mobile 'I think there are burglars in my house.'

She waited outside. A few minutes later a police car arrived with two police officers. Jill opened the front door again. One of the police officers pushed the living room door and looked in the room. Then he laughed.

Jill looked in the room, too. 'Peter,' she shouted. 'What are you doing here?' There weren't any burglars in the room. The TV was on and Jill's son, Peter, was asleep on the sofa.

'I arrived at half past one, but nobody was in,' Peter explained later. 'I decided to come home for Mum's birthday as a surprise. It was certainly a surprise when I opened my eyes, and the police were there. It was very embarrassing for Mum, but the police officers laughed about it.'

a Choose the correct answers.

1 Who had a birthday?
a Faith b Peter c Jill d Harry

2 What were *the voices*?
a burglars b Jill's friends c Peter's friends d the TV

b Who are the people? Choose the correct descriptions.

1 Faith is *Jill's sister / Jill's friend*.

2 Harry is *Jill's husband / Jill's brother*.

3 Peter is *Jill's son / a policeman*.

2 Are the statements true (T) or false (F)?

1 _F_ Jill's birthday was last Tuesday.
2 __ She was 50.
3 __ Jill and Faith were schoolfriends.
4 __ Jill travelled home by bus.
5 __ Peter is a student.
6 __ The voices were in the kitchen.
7 __ Peter phoned the police.
8 __ Two police officers arrived.
9 __ Peter came home because he needed money.
10 __ The police arrested Peter.

3 Put the sentences in the correct order and join them with *because*.

1 It was Jill's birthday. Faith invited Jill to lunch.
Faith invited Jill to lunch because it was Jill's birthday.

2 They were at school together. Faith and Jill were friends.
____
____

3 There were voices in the living room. Jill called the police.
____
____

4 There wasn't a burglar in the room. The police officers laughed.
____
____

5 It was his mum's birthday. Peter came home.
____
____

6 The TV was on. There were voices in the living room.
____
____

72 Talking about dates
Review: lessons 69–72

1 Complete the names of the months.

Jan*uary*
________uary
Ma_____
______il
M____
____ne
Ju____
______ust
Sept__________
________ber
Nov__________
______ember

2 Write the ordinal numbers.

1 **24th** *twenty-fourth*
2 **2nd** *second*
3 **16th** ________
4 **28th** ________
5 **31st** ________
6 **9th** ________
7 **20th** ________
8 **10th** ________
9 **30th** ________
10 **23rd** ________

3 How do you say the dates? Complete the phrases.

Birthdays

1 Simone – 1 Oct	6 Dad – 3 Nov
2 Mum – 7 Apr	7 Pete – 22 Aug
3 Vital – 14 May	8 Carol – 19 Mar
4 Sanjay – 30 Sept	9 Kuldeep – 12 Jul
5 Mirka – 21 Feb	10 Ollie – 20 Dec

1 *the first of October*
2 the ________ of ________
3 ________ May
4 ____ thirtieth ________
5 ________
6 ________ of ________
7 ________
8 the ________
9 ________
10 ________ of ________

Lessons 69–72

Choose the correct sentences.

1 a I start work at nine o'clock yesterday.
  b I started work at nine o'clock yesterday.
2 a I was late because there was an accident.
  b I was late because it was an accident.
3 a Help! Call the fire brigade.
  b Help! Call a fire brigade.
4 a She's a police officer.
  b She's police officer.
5 a The accident stoped all the cars.
  b The accident stopped all the cars.
6 a I phoned my parents yesterday.
  b I phond my parents yesterday.
7 a Our meeting is on the ninth of september.
  b Our meeting is on the ninth of September.
8 a My birthday is on second March.
  b My birthday is on the second of March.

✓ Now ... *review your progress.*

73 Irregular past forms
Writing: your day yesterday

1 Look at the infinitive and past forms. Are the verbs regular (R) or irregular (I)?

Present	Past	I / R
1 come	came	I
2 drink	drank	R
3 finish	finished	
4 leave	left	
5 send	sent	
6 write	wrote	
7 cook	cooked	
8 eat	ate	

Present	Past	I / R
9 go	went	
10 move	moved	
11 stop	stopped	
12 close	closed	
13 find	found	
14 like	liked	
15 read	read	
16 watch	watched	

2 Look at the wordsquare. Find the past simple of the irregular verbs in the box.

~~drive~~ come buy make leave write find take
have drink go do see eat get

A	L	E	F	T	W	Z	G	N	W	X	W
P	B	E	A	W	M	B	O	B	O	Q	R
R	C	N	H	A	D	T	T	F	A	F	O
D	R	A	N	K	U	C	V	Z	D	V	T
K	L	Q	S	L	B	O	U	G	H	T	E
W	J	M	D	C	Y	E	C	X	K	E	R
E	M	A	P	I	J	E	D	O	V	R	K
N	R	D	E	F	D	J	A	O	A	L	T
T	D	E	Y	C	T	U	R	B	T	Z	O
I	G	S	D	G	X	D	I	H	E	G	O
B	C	A	M	E	I	S	A	W	B	Y	K
T	H	U	H	O	F	O	U	N	D	V	M

3 Write the past simple of the verbs.

1 arrive *arrived*
2 buy *bought*
3 do ________
4 drive ________
5 get ________
6 have ________
7 help ________
8 make ________
9 need ________
10 phone ________
11 play ________
12 see ________
13 start ________
14 take ________
15 travel ________
16 wait ________

4 Put the verbs in brackets into the past simple.

On Sunday morning I [1] *got up* (get up) at 9.30 and I [2] ________ (go) out for some milk and a newspaper. On the way to the shop, I [3] ________ (meet) my friend, Josie. We [4] ________ (decide) to go to the beach later. I [5] ________ (see) Ella and Pedro in the shop, so I [6] ________ (invite) them, too.

At 11.30, everyone [7] ________ (come) to my flat. We [8] ________ (put) our things in the car and [9] ________ (drive) to the beach. We [10] ________ (arrive) at about one o'clock, so we [11] ________ (get) some sandwiches and drinks and we [12] ________ (eat) them. After lunch we [13] ________ (sit) on the beach. Then we [14] ________ (play) volleyball and we [15] ________ (swim) in the sea. It [16] ________ (be) a bit cold, but it was fun.

We [17] ________ (leave) at about six o'clock. We [18] ________ (have) a great time.

5 Write sentences about your day yesterday. Use the cues.

1 *I got up late.* OR *I got up at 7.30.*

1 I ________ (get up)
2 I ________ (go)
3 I ________ (have)
4 I ________ (see)
5 I ________ (buy)
6 I ________ (listen to)
7 I ________ (eat)
8 I ________ (watch)
9 I ________ (finish)
10 I ________ (drink)

✓ **Now ...** *practise and learn.*

74 Past simple: negative statements
Pronunciation: sentence stress

1 Make the sentences negative.

1 I woke up early this morning.
I *didn't wake up* early this morning.

2 We took the train to Paris.
We ________________ the train to Paris.

3 She finished work at 5.30 yesterday.
She ________________ work at 5.30 yesterday.

4 You sent those emails.
You ________________ those emails.

5 They liked the meal.
They ________________ the meal.

6 It rained yesterday.
It ________________ yesterday.

7 Sofia went to Paris
Sofia ________________ to Paris.

8 Tina bought a new car.
Tina ________________ a new car.

2 Complete two past simple sentences about each picture. Use the cues.

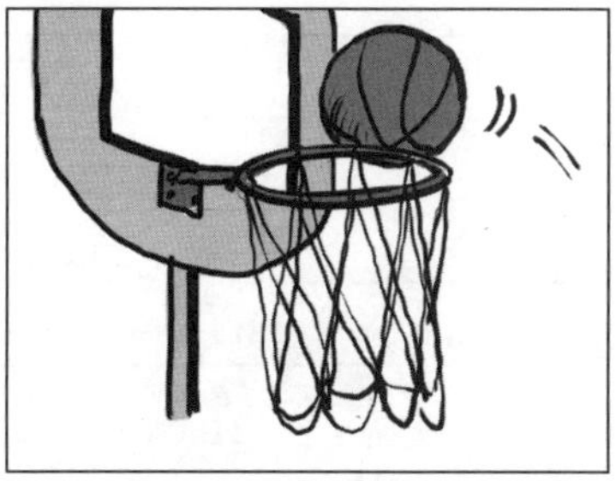

1 play football / play basketball
We *didn't play football*.
We *played basketball*.

2 go skating / go skiing
They ________________.
They ________________.

3 take the bus / take a taxi
He ________________.
He ________________.

4 buy some clothes / buy a TV
She ________________.
She ________________.

3 Choose the correct sentences.

1 a I don't go to work yesterday.
b I didn't go to work yesterday. ✓

2 a You didn't clean the windows.
b You didn't cleaned the windows.

3 a He buyed a book.
b He bought a book.

4 a We didn't have breakfast.
b We no had breakfast.

5 a She didn't leave at 10.30.
b She didn't left at 10.30.

6 a They didn't were at the party.
b They weren't at the party.

4 Complete the sentences about yourself. Use the past simple of the verbs.

1 I went out last night. OR
I didn't go out last night.

1 I ________________ last night. (go out)

2 I ________________ a taxi yesterday. (take)

3 I ________________ a new mobile phone last year. (buy)

4 I ________________ TV last night. (watch)

5 I ________________ an English lesson yesterday. (have)

6 I ________________ a fire engine this morning. (see)

7 I ________________ an email yesterday. (write)

8 I ________________ jeans last Sunday. (wear)

5 Pronunciation Mark the two stressed syllables in each sentence.

1 They went to the cinema.

2 I didn't have lunch.

3 We bought a new car.

4 He didn't play tennis.

5 She got up late.

6 We stayed at home.

75 Reading and writing: a biography
Ages and life stages

1 Read the text.

My name's Teresa. I was born in Argentina. We lived in a suburb of Buenos Aires. When I was four, we left Argentina and we moved to Spain. My father worked for an engineering company in Bilbao, and my mother worked in a hospital.

I went to school in Bilbao. I liked school. I was good at languages. But I didn't like sport. We played tennis, but I wasn't very good at it. After school, I went to university in Madrid. I studied English and French. I really enjoyed university, and I made a lot of new friends.

After university I moved to Australia. I worked in a hotel in Sydney. It was hard work, but I learned a lot of English. Then I got a good job with an international sports company. I thought that was funny, because I don't like sport.

I went to lots of sports events with my job. I met my husband, Callum, at a rugby match. He played for one of the teams. We got married two years later. We've got two children now. Our daughter, Mona, is three years old and our son, Lucas, was born in November last year.

a Find the names of the people.

1 *Teresa* the woman in the photograph
2 ________ her husband
3 ________ her daughter
4 ________ her son

b Number the places in the order that Teresa lived in them.

__ Bilbao
__ Sydney
1 Buenos Aires
__ Madrid

2 Read the text again. Match the parts of the sentences.

1 Teresa was born __ a in Bilbao.
2 Her family moved __ b to Australia.
3 Her school was __ c at a rugby match.
4 She studied at university __ d a sports company.
5 After university she went __ e to Spain.
6 She worked in a hotel __ f in Argentina.
7 She got a good job with __ g in Madrid.
8 She met her husband __ h in Sydney.

3 Complete the sentences about your life.

1 I was born in ______________________,
in ______________________. (*town, country?*)
2 My parents worked (*in / for*) ______________________
______________________.
3 I went to ______________________ School.
4 I ______________________ school. (*liked?*)
5 I ______________________ sport. (*liked?*)
6 When I left school I ______________________
______________________. (*studies / job?*)

✓ **Now ...** ***practise and learn.***

4 When do people do these things in your country? Write the ages.

_____ Children start school.
_____ You can leave school.
_____ All students leave school.
_____ You can drive a car.
_____ You can get married.
_____ Most students start university.
_____ Most students leave university.

76 Saying who is right and wrong
Review: lessons 73–76

1 Put the expressions in the correct order.

1 right was Lucy

____

2 Ryan's was it fault

____

3 my wasn't fault it

____

2 Complete the sentences.

1 I didn't do it. John did it.

It wasn't __my__ fault.

It was __John's__ fault.

2 It wasn't ________ fault.

It was ________ fault.

He didn't do it. She did it.

3 Kirsty didn't do it. Tim did it.

It wasn't ________ fault.

It was ________ fault.

4 It wasn't ________ fault.

It was ________ fault.

We didn't do it. They did it.

5 The girl didn't do it. The boy did it.

It wasn't the ________ fault.

It was the ________ fault.

3 Complete the conversation. Use the past simple of the verbs.

Jordan Lucy still isn't talking to me. She was at The Coffee Shop yesterday. But she [1] __left__ (leave) when she [2] ____________ (see) me.

Peter Oh dear. And Cindy's still angry with Ryan, too.

Jordan Yes, because you [3] ____________ (tell) Cindy.

Peter Hey, it [4] ____________ (not be) my fault.

Jordan Yes, you're right. It [5] ____________ (be) Ryan's fault.

Peter Come on, Jordan. You [6] ____________ (go) to the match, too.

Jordan Yes, I know. But I [7] ____________ (try) to phone Lucy. And I [8] ____________ (send) a text.

Peter But her phone wasn't working.

Jordan Yes, but I [9] ____________ (not know) that. So why is she angry?

Peter Look. Lucy [10] ____________ (want) to go to the rock concert with her friends, but she [11] ____________ (not go), because she [12] ____________ (have) a date with you. But you …

Jordan I [13] ____________ (go) to the football match. Yes, Lucy was right. I am an idiot.

Lessons 73–76

Choose the correct sentences.

1 a I didn't went to work yesterday.
  b I didn't go to work yesterday.

2 a She was born in India.
  b She's born in India.

3 a He was reporter.
  b He was a reporter.

4 a They didn't go to university.
  b They no went to university.

5 a I wasn't at home last night.
  b I didn't was at home last night.

6 a We don't play basketball last week.
  b We didn't play basketball last week.

7 a She writed a letter yesterday.
  b She wrote a letter yesterday.

8 a I didn't cook the dinner.
  b I didn't cooked the dinner.

✓ Now … *review your progress.*

77 Weekend activities
Writing: last weekend

1 Match the parts of the expressions.

1 meet _d_ — a the car
2 pay ___ — b in the garden
3 go ___ — c the washing
4 wash ___ — d our friends
5 visit ___ — e to the park
6 tidy ___ — f the bills
7 do ___ — g my family
8 work ___ — h the living room

2 Make sentences about their weekend activities. Use the expressions in exercise 1 in the past simple.

1 Tom _went to the park_.

2 Ana ________________.

3 Adrien ________________.

4 I ________________.

5 Sam ________________.

6 Victor ________________.

7 David ________________.

8 We ________________.

3 Solve the anagrams and write the words.

1 I visited my p_a r e n t_s. (sanpret)

2 We went to the ___h______r___. (heettra)

3 I went ______pp______. (nipoghsp)

4 We relaxed in the _____r_____n. (negrad)

5 I went to the c_______m___. (menaic)

6 We played frisbee in the __________. (karp)

7 I met my _____i______s. (drefins)

8 I tidied the _____us___. (eshou)

4 Complete the sentences about your weekend. Use the past simple of the verbs.

Last weekend

1 I _went_ OR _didn't go_ to the cinema. (go)

2 I ____________ the bills. (pay)

3 I ____________ the washing. (do)

4 I ____________ my friends at a restaurant. (meet)

5 I ____________ my room. (tidy)

6 I ____________ my family. (visit)

7 I ____________ the car. (wash)

8 I ____________ in front of the TV. (relax)

✓ Now ... *practise and learn.*

78 Past simple: questions
Writing: a conversation about your weekend

1 Complete the conversations. Use the words and expressions in the boxes.

1 had (×2) didn't have ~~did ... have~~

A [1] *Did* you *have* a good weekend?

B Yes, I did. I [2]________ a very nice time. What about you?

A No, I [3]________ a good weekend. I [4]________ toothache.

B Oh dear.

2 did ... go went (×2) didn't go

A We [1]________ to the beach at the weekend.

B Oh, [2]________ you ________ in your new car?

A No, we [3]________ by car. We [4]________ by train.

3 didn't make did ... make made (×2)

A This is nice soup. [1]________ you ________ it?

B No, I didn't. Emma [2]________ it. I [3]________ the sandwiches, either. Daniel [4]________ them.

2 Complete the conversation. Use short answers.

1 **A** Did you go shopping on Saturday?

B Yes, *I did*.

A Did Maria go with you?

B No, ________.

2 **A** Did your parents go to Spain for their holiday?

B No, ________. They went to France.

A Did they drive?

B Yes, ________.

3 **A** Did you go to the cinema last night?

B No, ________. We went to the theatre.

A Did you enjoy the play?

B Yes, ________.

4 **A** Did your brother visit last weekend?

B Yes, ________.

A Did you have a good time?

B Yes, ________.

3 Make questions.

1 Kelly visited her family.

Did Kelly visit her family?

2 You cleaned the windows.

________ the windows?

3 We left at quarter to five.

________ at quarter to five?

4 Bill found his wallet.

________ his wallet?

5 It rained yesterday.

________ yesterday?

4 Write about your weekend.

a Complete the questions. Use the past simple of the verbs.

b Make short answers about yourself.

1 **A** *Did you have* a good weekend? (have)

You *Yes, I did.* OR *No, I didn't.*

2 **A** ________ any new clothes? (buy)

You ________

3 **A** ________ to the cinema? (go)

You ________

4 **A** ________ the washing? (do)

You ________

5 **A** ________ your friends? (meet)

You ________

6 **A** ________ TV? (watch)

You ________

✓ **Now ...** *practise and learn.*

79 Reading and writing: last weekend

1 Complete the conversation. Choose the correct words.

Mark Did you [1]*have* / ~~*had*~~ a good weekend?
Adam It was OK.
Mark What did you [2]*do* / *did*?
Adam Well, on Saturday morning I [3]*go* / *went* into town and I [4]*pay* / *paid* some bills. I [5]*meet* / *met* some friends for lunch.
Mark Oh, yes. Where did you [6]*go* / *went*?
Adam Oh, we [7]*go* / *went* to a pub and we [8]*watch* / *watched* a rugby match on TV there. What about you? Did you [9]*have* / *had* a good weekend?
Mark Not really, I [10]*want* / *wanted* to watch the rugby match on Saturday, but I [11]*go* / *went* shopping with my girlfriend, Emma.
Adam Did you [12]*buy* / *bought* anything?
Mark No, I didn't. Emma [13]*buy* / *bought* one or two things. I [14]*look* / *looked* at some really nice jackets, but I [15]*didn't buy* / *bought* one.
Adam Oh, OK.
Mark What did you [16]*do* / *did* on Sunday?
Adam I [17]*didn't do* / *did* a lot. I [18]*tidy* / *tidied* my flat. Then I [19]*relax* / *relaxed* in front of the TV. What about you?
Mark We [20]*visit* / *visited* Emma's parents.

2 Put the words in the correct order to make questions.

1 did where go you ?
Where did you go?

2 they did what time arrive ?
____

3 travel how did you ?
____

4 did meet she who ?
____

5 the concert when finish did ?
____

6 you buy did what ?
____

7 did he leave why ?
____

8 where did have lunch you ?
____

3a Complete the questions. Use the cues.

b Answer the questions about yourself.

1 What time *did you get up* today? (you / get up)
I got up at six o'clock.

2 What ______________ for breakfast? (you / have)
____

3 What ______________ on TV last night? (you / watch)
____

4 What ______________ last Saturday morning? (you / do)
____

5 What ______________ last Sunday? (you / do)
____

6 Where ______________ on your last holiday? (you / go)
____

7 What time ______________ to bed last night? (you / go)
____

8 How ______________ to work / school? (you / travel)
____

✓ Now ... *practise and learn.*

80 Time prepositions, building a conversation
Review: lessons 77–80

1 Complete the table. Use the expressions in the box.

the afternoon	12th March	the evening
six thirty	Monday afternoon	night

***at* + times**	half past nine, the weekend, ______ ______
***in* + parts of the day**	the morning, ______ ______
***on* + • days • parts of specific days • dates**	Saturday, ______ ______

2 Number the conversation in the correct order.

a __ Did you enjoy it?
b __ We went to *The Peacock.*
c __ Yes, we did. the food was very good.
d __ Where did you go?
e *1* We went to a restaurant.
f __ What did you do last night?

3 Complete the conversation. Use the correct past form of the verbs.

A What [1]______ you ______ on Friday? (do)
B We [2]______ to the cinema. (go)
A What [3]______ you ______? (see)
B We [4]______ *African Sky.* (see)
A [5]______ it good? (be)
B No, it [6]______ . The actors [7]______ terrible.
I [8]______ the film at all!
(not be / be / not like)

4 Make the conversation. Use the cues.

A What / do / on Saturday?
What did you do on Saturday?
B We / go / to the beach
______
A Who / you / go / with?
______
B I / go / with my family
______
A weather / good?
______
B Yes / be
______

Lessons 77–80

Choose the correct sentences.

1 a We went to the park in Sunday afternoon.
b We went to the park on Sunday afternoon.
2 a Did you take the train?
b Did you took the train?
3 a What you did at the weekend?
b What did you do at the weekend?
4 a Did you tidy the house?
b Did you the house tidy ?
5 a Where you went yesterday?
b Where did you go yesterday?
6 a Did the film was good?
b Was the film good?
7 a We went to the cinema last night.
b We went the cinema last night.
8 a I lost my mobile yesterday.
b I losed my mobile yesterday.

✓ Now ... *review your progress.*

Workbook key

1

1 1 Hello 2 My 3 Pleased 4 meet 5 I'm 6 Nice 7 you 8 your 9 surname

2 1 I'm Irena. 2 What's your name? 3 My name's Mike. 4 I'm Pedro. 5 My surname's Hall.

3

						[1]S	I	X	
						E			
						V			
			[2]F	I	V	E			[3]Z
	[4]T	W	O			[5]N	I	N	E
			U						R
	[6]T	H	R	[7]E	E				O
	E			I					
[8]O	N	E		G					
				H					
				T					

4 1 Home 01726 225899 Mobile 07795 892433
2 Home 020 611 7095 Mobile 07920 566448

5 Students' own answers.

6 Students' own answers.

2

1

							[1]U		
							[2]M	A	N
							B		
			[3]B	[4]O	Y		R		
				R			E		
				[5]A	P	P	L	E	
[6]W	O	M	A	N			L		
				G		[7]B	A	[8]G	
[9]H	O	U	S	E				I	
						[10]C	A	R	
								L	

2 ***a***
a chair
a book
a pencil
a table
a pen
a computer

an + a/e/i/o/u
an apple
an eraser
an umbrella
an orange

3 1 this 2 that 3 That 4 This 5 This 6 That

4 **1** 1 does 2 mean 3 means
2 1 do 2 English 3 say

3

1 1 window 2 teacher 3 board 4 door 5 desk 6 notebook 7 book 8 student 9 pen 10 chair

2 1 b 2 a 3 b 4 a 5 b 6 a

3 1 don't know 2 can, repeat 3 sorry, understand

4

1 1 L 2 P 3 H 4 A 5 B 6 E 7 T
ALPHABET

2 1 your 2 name 3 My name's 4 How 5 spell 6 double 7 Thank you

3 1 this 2 meet 3 Nice 4 sorry 5 name 6 My

4 1 Tea or coffee, Marco? 2 Tea, please. 3 Here you are. 4 Thanks, Ivana.

Review: Lessons 1–4
1 My 2 to 3 does 4 Don't 5 your 6 is 7 an 8 I'm

5

1

	M	O	T	[1]H	E	R				
		D	A	[2]U	G	H	T	E	R	
		S	I	[3]S	T	E	R			
				[4]B	R	O	T	H	E	R
			F	[5]A	T	H	E	R		
P	A	R	E	[6]N	T	S				
C	H	I	L	[7]D	R	E	N			

2 1 daughter, father 2 wifew, husband 3 son, mother 4 parents, children

3 1 Daniel's 2 Donna Mancini's 3 Pavel, Jitka's 4 Laura's

4 1 That is Helen's husband.
2 He is Maria's friend.
3 She is Jim's wife.
4 What is Miguel's number?
5 Sarah is here.
6 What is Peter's surname?

6

1 1 his, his 2 her, his, her 3 Her, her, His

2 1 My, your, My 2 her, Her, her, his, His 3 your, his, my, her 4 my, our, Its

3 1 our 2 Its 3 His 4 his 5 Her 6 their 7 Their

7

1 1 a Yves b Sonia c Véronique d Philippe e Bruno
2 a Marek b Jola c Jacek d Ewa

2 1 parents 2 dad, His 3 mum, Her 4 wife, Her 5 My 6 brother, His 7 children, Their

3 Students' own answers.

4 /aɪ/ nine, wife
/ɑː/ are, car
/iː/ he, read
/e/ friend, ten

8

1 1 *Goodbye* and *See you* are incorrect.
2 *Good evening* and *Hi* are incorrect.

2 1 b 2 d 3 c 4 f 5 a 6 e

3 1 b 2 a 3 b 4 b

Review: Lessons 5–8
1 e 2 d 3 h 4 a 5 g 6 b 7 f 8 c

9

1 a 1 Britain 2 France 3 Russia 4 Spain 5 Japan 6 the USA 7 Italy 8 China 9 Brazil 10 Egypt 11 Indonesia 12 Australia
b Students' own answers.

2 1 Cairo is the capital of Egypt.
2 Sydney is in Australia.
3 My favourite country is China.
4 My favourite city is New York.
5 Is Antonio from Spain?
6 My home is in Poland.
7 Rome is the capital of Italy.
8 He's from Argentina.

3 Students' own answers.

4 1 Hungary 2 Korea 3 Australia 4 Brazil 5 Russia 6 Japan 7 Italy 8 America 9 Indonesia 10 Britain

10

1 1 I am from France.
2 John is a student.
3 Moscow is in Russia.
4 We are from China.
5 My friends are from Italy.
6 She is my daughter.
7 My husband is from the USA.
8 I am a teacher.

2 1 We are students.
2 I am from New York.
3 They are his friends.
4 She is from Greece.
5 Dan is my husband.
6 I am her sister.
7 Manchester is in the UK.
8 You are in Room 9.

3 1 She isn't the Managing Director.
2 I'm not at my desk.
3 This isn't my mobile.
4 They aren't brother and sister.
5 We aren't from Shanghai.
6 Lukas isn't in his office.
7 I'm not married.
8 You aren't in this photo.
9 My boss isn't here.
10 Our children aren't here.

4 Students' own answers.

11

1 a 1 I'm a student.
2 She isn't a teacher.
3 He's a doctor.
4 My sister's an engineer.
5 You're a student.
6 I'm a computer engineer.

b 1 I'm a student and I'm from Russia.
2 She isn't a teacher and she isn't from China.
3 He's a doctor and he's from South Africa.
4 My sister's an engineer and she's from the Czech Republic.
5 You're a student and you're from Italy.
6 I'm a computer engineer and I'm from Brazil.

2 1 He's 2 His 3 He's 4 his 5 He's 6 He's, his

3 a 1 Japan 2 an English teacher 3 Daisuke 4 Haru's boyfriend 5 Australia 6 a doctor 7 an engineer 8 Jane's husband

b 1 Haru's from Japan and she's an English teacher. She's Daisuke's girlfriend.
2 Daisuke's from the USA and he's a student. He's Haru's boyfriend.
3 Jane's from Australia and she's a doctor. She's Dieter's wife.
4 Dieter's from Germany and he's an engineer. He's Jane's husband.

4 Students' own answers.

12

1 a 1 d 2 a 3 c 4 b
  b 1 very sorry 2 you OK 3 all right
    4 fine

2 1 Ow. My hand! 4 Are you OK?
  2 Oh, I'm very sorry. 5 Yes, I'm fine, thank you.
  3 It's all right.

Review: Lessons 9–12
1 I'm from Russia.
2 She's a doctor.
3 He's in the office.
4 I'm not married.
5 He's from the USA.
6 They're from France.
7 This is John's phone.
8 We aren't in Room 10.
9 This is a book.
10 Your desk's over there.

13

1 thirty, sixty-five, fifty, nineteen, ninety-eight, fifty-three, twenty-four, eighty-one, sixty, thirteen, seventy-seven, forty-two

2 a 2 two 20 twenty 13 thirteen 4 four 40 forty 15 fifteen 6 six 60 sixty 17 seventeen 8 eight 80 eighty 19 nineteen

b thirteen	eighteen	sixty
fourteen	nineteen	seventy
fifteen	thirty	eighty
sixteen	forty	ninety
seventeen	fifty	

3 1 twenty-one 2 fifty-two 3 eighty-six 4 twelve 5 eleven 6 ninety-one 7 forty-five 8 fourteen 9 a hundred 10 sixty-eight 11 thirty-three 12 seventy-nine

4 1 e 2 d 3 a 4 b 5 f 6 c

5 Students' own answers.

14

1 1 Are you 3 Is that 5 Are they
  2 Is he 4 Are we 6 Are you

2 1 Yes, he is. 4 No, it isn't.
  2 No, we aren't. 5 Yes, I am.
  3 No, they aren't.

3 1 isn't 2 isn't 3 am 4 is 5 aren't 6 are

4 1 How old is Juan?
  2 Where are they from?
  3 Where is your office?
  4 How old are your children?
  5 What is her name?
  6 What is his phone number?

5 Students' own answers.

6 Students' own answers.

15

1 a old b first c from d your e Are f What's

2 1 What's your surname?
  2 What's your first name?
  3 Where are you from?
  4 How old are you?
  5 Are you married?
  6 What's your phone number?

3 f Surname b First name c Country a Age e Marital status d Tel. No.

4 a

Information	**Anita**
Surname	Moretti
First name	Anita
Country	Italy
Age	twenty-four
Marital status	single
Tel. No.	0209 736 522

  b Students' own answers.

5 1 What's your surname?
  2 Students' own answers.
  3 What's your first name?
  4 Students' own answers.
  5 And where are you from?
  6 Students' own answers.
  7 How old are you, please?
  8 Students' own answers.
  9 Are you married?
  10 Students' own answers.
  11 And what's your phone number, please?
  12 Students' own answers.

16

1 1 c 2 f 3 b 4 e 5 d 6 a

2 1 It's twenty to twelve.
  2 It's quarter past one.
  3 It's seven o'clock.
  4 It's twenty-five to six.
  5 It's twenty past eight.
  6 It's ten to five.

3 Students' own answers.

Review: Lessons 13–16
1 f 2 d 3 e 4 g 5 c 6 b 7 h 8 a

17

1

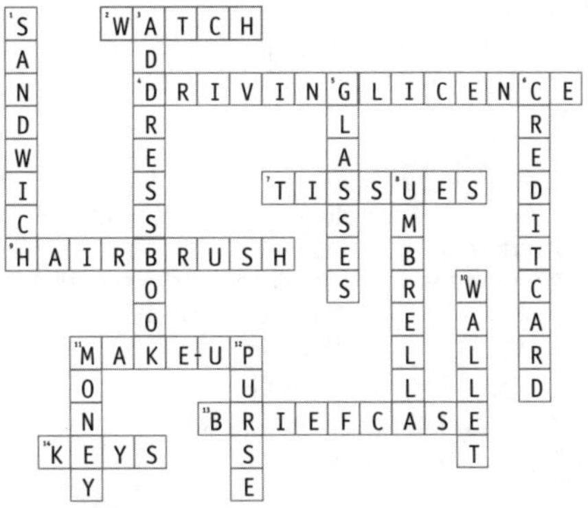

2 1 a wallet 2 dogs 3 a child 4 a woman 5 a watch 6 men 7 a hairbrush 8 keys 9 a sandwich 10 a person

3 Students' own answers.

4 a and b

Singular (syllables)	**Plural (syllables)**	**Extra syllable?**
1 pencil (2)	pencils (2)	
2 watch (1)	watches (2)	✓
3 briefcase (2)	briefcases (3)	✓
4 umbrella (3)	umbrellas (3)	
5 apple (2)	apples (2)	
6 purse (1)	purses (2)	✓
7 tissue (2)	tissues (2)	
8 licence (2)	licences (3)	✓
9 orange (2)	oranges (3)	✓
10 key (1)	keys (1)	

18

1 1 d 2 c 3 e 4 a 5 f 6 b

2 1 next to 2 in 3 behind 4 on 5 in front of 6 under

3 1 an, a, The, the 3 an, a, The, the
  2 a, a, The, the 4 a, a, The, the

19

1 1 b 2 d 3 g 4 f 5 c 6 h 7 e 8 a

2 1 this 2 those 3 that 4 those 5 that 6 those

3 a 1 Can I help you?
    2 How much are those wallets?
    3 Can I have that one, please?
    4 Anything else?
  b 1 Can I help you?
    2 How much are these bags?
    3 They're £28 each.
    4 Can I have this one, please?
    5 Certainly.
    6 Anything else?
    7 No, thank you.

4 1 Push 2 Pull 3 Open 4 Closed 5 Exit 6 Toilet

20

1 1 f 2 c 3 d 4 e 5 a 6 b

2 1 b 2 a 3 e 4 c 5 d

3 a 1 to, can't, you
    2 off, you, for
  b 1 1 We're 2 the café 3 you coming 4 sorry 5 can't 6 OK 7 you later
    2 1 I'm off to The Coffee Shop.
      2 Are you coming?
      3 Yes, but only for a few minutes.
      4 Great.

Review: Lessons 17–20

1 help	4 boxes	7 That's
2 those	5 They're	8 Here you are
3 in front of	6 have	9 change

A Hello. Can I help you?
B Yes, How much are those bags, please?
A The bags in front of the window?
B No, the bags next to the boxes.
A They're £26.
B Can I have this one, please?
A That's £26, then, please.
B Here you are.
A Thank you. That's £4 change.

21

1

Food		**Drinks**	
meat	fish	tea	orange juice
apples	cheese	wine	beer
noodles	bread	milk	water
vegetables	eggs	coffee	

2

1 fruit	6 butter
2 rice	7 meat
3 chips	8 eggs
4 chocolate	9 vegetables
5 pasta	10 fish

3 Students' own answers.

4

Voiced		**Voiceless**	
bread	cheese	butter	chips
eggs	beer	fruit	juice
vegetables	lemonade	chocolate	water

22

1 1 I like chocolate. 2 We don't eat fish. 3 They like fruit. 4 I don't drink beer. 5 They eat rice. 6 We don't like cheese. 7 I like fruit. 8 They don't drink tea.

2 1 They don't drink milk.
2 I don't like this restaurant.
3 We don't eat apples and oranges.
4 You don't drink wine.
5 We don't like cheese sandwiches.
6 They don't drink tea in the morning.
7 I don't like sport.
8 They don't eat meat.

3 1 drink tea, don't drink coffee
2 eat rice, don't eat pasta
3 like dogs, don't like cats
4 don't drink wine, drink beer
5 eat bread, don't eat rice
6 like books, don't like TV

4 Students' own answers.

23

1

```
     ¹BREAD
BUTTE²R
   CH³EESE
  POT⁴ATOES
 CHIC⁵KEN
     ⁶FISH
  CRE⁷AM
     ⁸SOUP
  MEA⁹T
```

2 1 I eat fruit, but I don't eat apples.
2 We don't drink coffee, but we drink tea.
3 They eat bananas, but they don't eat oranges.
4 We don't drink milk, but we drink water.
5 They like meat, but they don't like fish.
6 I eat lunch, but I don't eat breakfast.

3 1 dinner 2 breakfast 3 dessert 4 lunch

4 Students' own answers.

24

1 1 water 2 cup 3 glass 4 ice 5 lemon 6 sugar

2 1 e 2 c 3 a 4 b 5 d

3 a 1 like 2 please 3 thank 4 are 5 welcome
b 1 Would you like 2 please 3 please 4 you are 5 Thank 6 You're welcome

Review: Lessons 21–24
1 b 2 b 3 a 4 b 5 a 6 b 7 a 8 b

25

1 1 shopping 2 swimming 3 TV 4 karate 5 novels 6 the radio 7 music 8 football 9 tennis

2 1 watch, listen to, read, do
2 play, go, go
3 listen to, watch, play, do
4 go, read, do, play

3 1 either 2 too 3 too 4 either 5 too 6 either 7 too 8 either

4 Students' own answers.

26

1 1 Do you play tennis?
2 Do you like music?
3 Do you go swimming?
4 Do you listen to the radio?
5 Do you eat fish?
6 Do you do karate?
7 Do you read a newspaper?
8 Do you watch DVDs?
9 Do you drink tea?
10 Do you play computer games?

2 1 do 2 don't 3 don't 4 do 5 do 6 don't

3 a 1 Do you 2 Do you 3 Do you 4 Do you 5 Do you 6 Do you
b Students' own answers.

4 1 disk 2 cursor 3 mouse 4 screen 5 monitor 6 keyboard

27

1 1 Yes 2 Yes 3 Yes 4 No 5 Yes 6 Yes 7 Yes 8 No

2 Students' own answers.

3

Short vowels	**Long vowels**
/ɪ/ drink	/iː/ eat
/ɒ/ novel	/ɔː/ sport
/ʊ/ good	/uː/ you
/æ/ cat	/ɑː/ car
/ə/ karate	/ɜː/ purse

28

1 1 d 2 b 3 a 4 c

2 1 d 2 b 3 e 4 f 5 a 6 c

3 1 off 2 I'm 3 to 4 lift

4 PRIVATE NO PARKING

Review: Lessons 25–28
1 play 2 Do 3 to 4 do 5 go 6 do 7 like 8 don't

29

1 1 a 2 b 3 a 4 a 5 b 6 b

2

I live	alone, with my parents
I live in a	flat
My home is in	a small town, the suburbs
I	take the bus, walk
… to	school

3 1 alone, flat, centre, walk
2 family, house, suburbs, drive

4 Students' own answers.

30

1 1 a i b ii 2 a ii b i 3 a i b ii 4 a i b ii 5 a ii b i 6 a i b ii 7 a ii b i 8 a i b ii

2 1 When do you go swimming?
2 What time do they have dinner?
3 Where do they play tennis?
4 How do you go to school?
5 What do you eat for breakfast?
6 Where do you have lunch?
7 What do you do in your free time?
8 What time do the shops open?

3 1 do you live 2 do you live 3 do you work 4 do you go 5 do you have 6 do you do 7 do you go

4 Students' own answers.

31

1 their names their home work free time

2 1 like 2 city centre 3 flat 4 at the university 5 walk 6 run in marathons 7 marathons 8 concerts

3 1 Factory Road 2 Oxford Street 3 West Avenue 4 City Road

4 1 75 Factory Rd. 2 10 Ash St. 3 60 China Ave. 4 80 South Rd.

5 1 Mr Winston Deane
15 East Rd.
Manchester
M6 8LV

2 Ms I. Lovett
87 London St.
Cambridge
CB9 4RT

32

1 Monday Tuesday Wednesday Thursday Friday Saturday Sunday

2 1 Is Anna's party on Friday?
No, it isn't.
2 What time's your appointment at the doctor's?
It's at two o'clock.
3 Where's Suchart from?
He's from Thailand.
4 When's Johan's driving test?
It's on Tuesday.

3 1 on 2 at, on 3 on, an 4 at, on, on 5 on, at 6 at, at

Review: Lessons 29–32
1 a 2 b 3 a 4 b 5 b 6 b 7 a 8 a

33

1 a 1 i 2 a 3 e 4 c 5 h 6 d 7 f 8 b 9 g
b 1 wake up 2 get up 3 have a shower 4 have breakfast 5 go to work 6 start work 7 finish work 8 go home 9 go to bed

2 Students' own answers.

3 a Students' own answers.
b Students' own answers.

34

1 1 shares 2 works 3 watches 4 plays 5 does 6 goes

2 1 doesn't live 2 doesn't work 3 doesn't start 4 doesn't have 5 doesn't finish 6 doesn't do

3 1 work 2 works 3 lives 4 go 5 play 6 finishes 7 does 8 get up 9 take 10 drives

4 1 don't 2 doesn't 3 doesn't 4 don't 5 doesn't 6 don't 7 doesn't 8 don't

5 a and b

Verb (*I/You/We/They*)	**Verb + *-s/-es* (*He/She/It*)**	**Extra syllable?**
1 drive (1)	drives (1)	
2 finish (2)	finishes (3)	✓
3 do (1)	does (1)	
4 go (1)	goes (1)	
5 use (1)	uses (2)	✓
6 live (1)	lives (1)	
7 watch (1)	watches (2)	✓
8 take (1)	takes (1)	

35

1 1 Australia 2 with her husband 3 town 4 doctor 5 health centre 6 children

2 1 T 2 F 3 F 4 F 5 T 6 F 7 T 8 F

3 1 gets up 2 goes to work 3 starts work
4 finishes work 5 goes home 6 has dinner

4 a ***in* + parts of the day**
the evening, the morning
***on* + days**
Monday, Friday, Wednesday
***at* + times**
quarter to four, 10.25
b 1 at, in 2 in 3 in, in 4 on 5 at, in
6 on

36

1 1 c 2 e 3 a 4 b 5 d

2 1 I'm in a hurry 3 This is terrible
2 I'm late for a lesson 4 I'm in trouble

Review: Lessons 33–36
1 get up 2 works 3 goes 4 have
5 doesn't like 6 don't play 7 doesn't watch
8 in

37

1 1 secretary 2 waiter 3 nurse 4 chef
5 builder 6 shop assistant 7 housewife
8 mechanic 9 teacher 10 student
11 waitress 12 computer engineer

2

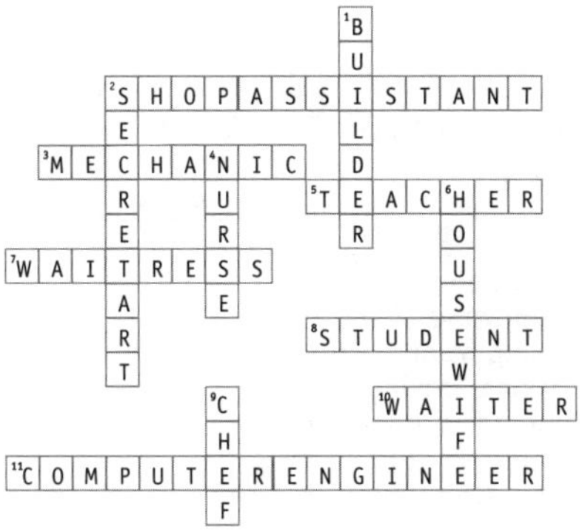

3 Students' own answers.

4 a 1 do 2 a 3 Where 4 What 5 teach
b Students' own answers.

38

1 1 do 2 Do 3 does 4 Does 5 Do
6 Does 7 do 8 do

2 1 does 2 don't 3 they do 4 don't
5 he doesn't 6 she does 7 do
8 she doesn't 9 they don't 10 do

3 1 Where does your daughter live?
2 What does she do?
3 Does she work in a hospital?
4 Where do they live?
5 Do they like Brussels?

4 a Students' own answers.
b Students' own answers.

39

1 1 a 2 c 3 a 4 c

2 a 1 What 2 How 3 Does 4 When
5 does 6 go 7 What 8 do 9 does
10 Does
b 1 He's a radio newsreader.
2 He drives.
3 No, he doesn't.
4 It starts at six o'clock.
5 It finishes at nine o'clock.
6 No, he doesn't.
7 He goes home at 11 o'clock.
8 He plays tennis and he goes to the cinema.
9 He works from Monday to Friday.
10 Yes, he does.

3 1 teacher 2 doctor 3 waiter 4 brother
5 newsreader 6 singer 7 reporter
8 builder

40

1 1 Do you live near here?
2 Where do you live?
3 What do you do?
4 Do you work for the local newspaper?
5 Do you like your job?
6 Where do you work?
7 What do you want to do?

2 1 T 2 T 3 F 4 F 5 F 6 F 7 T 8 F

3 1 Oh, right. 2 Me too. 3 That's interesting.
4 Really? 5 Oh, I see.

Review: Lessons 37–40
1 What do you do?
2 He's a builder.
3 Does she live in a city?
4 Does he like his job?
5 Where do you live?
6 No, she doesn't.
7 When do you finish work?
8 She wants to be a singer.

41

1 1 old 2 new 3 long 4 short 5 hot
6 cold 7 old 8 young 9 big 10 small

2 1 red 2 black 3 blue 4 orange
5 white 6 brown 7 yellow 8 green

3 1 b 2 a 3 a 4 b 5 a

4 1 blue cars 5 a red pen
2 a small village 6 a black car
3 a bad meal 7 a new computer
4 two young women 8 a cold drink

5 Students' own answers.

42

1 1 Jordan's got 2 We've got 3 I haven't got
4 She hasn't got 5 You've got
6 Anan's got 7 We haven't got
8 My office hasn't got

2 1 She hasn't got an umbrella.
2 They haven't got a new flat.
3 We haven't got a brown cat.
4 Lucy hasn't got a good boss.
5 You haven't got my mobile number.
6 We haven't got a meeting now.
7 He hasn't got an old computer.
8 I haven't got a young secretary.

3 1 b 2 b 3 a 4 b 5 b 6 a 7 b 8 b

4 a 1 He hasn't got an address book.
2 He's got a mobile.
3 He hasn't got a hairbrush.
4 He's got a wallet.
5 He's got a key.
6 He's got a pen.
b Students' own answers.

43

1 1 Tina 2 Ben 3 Ben

2 her new flat her flatmates
her new boss her parking space

3 1 F 2 F 3 T 4 F 5 F 6 T 7 T 8 F
9 F 10 F

4 1 d 2 f 3 b 4 e 5 c 6 a

5 1 b 2 a 3 d 4 e 5 f 6 c

44

1 1 b 2 d 3 e 4 a 5 c

2 1 Excuse me. Is this seat free?
Sure. Go ahead
2 Excuse me. Are these seats free?
No, I'm sorry. They're taken. Look! There's a table over there.

3 1 We've got a new neighbour.
2 Do you know my friend Gita?
3 Do you live near here?
4 I live in a block of flats.
5 My house is over there.
6 Carlos hasn't got long hair.
7 I don't work in London.
8 Sunita has got her own office.
9 My laptop is really fast.
10 We haven't got a new flat.
11 Bruno drives an old car.
12 Would you like a hot drink?

Review: Lessons 41–44
1 b 2 b 3 a 4 b 5 b 6 b 7 a 8 b

45

1

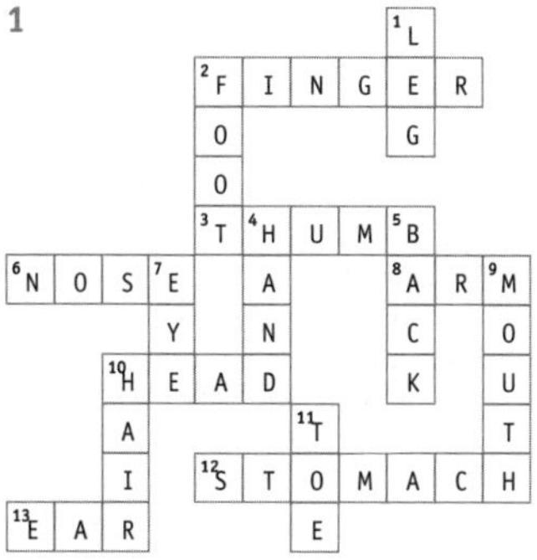

2 1 b 2 b 3 b 4 a 5 a 6 a

3 Students' own answers.

4 1 hair ear
2 back hand ✓
3 toe nose ✓
4 tooth mouth
5 hand arm
6 head leg ✓
7 thumb stomach ✓
8 feet eye

46

1 1 Have you got an aspirin?
2 Has she got a driving licence?
3 Have you got a cold?
4 Have they got a nice house?
5 Have we got a new boss?
6 Has Bill got a brother?
7 Have you got my keys?
8 Has Sonia got a boyfriend?

2 1 Have you got a newspaper?
2 Has Sandra got a new flat?
3 Have you got an email address?
4 Have we got a new neighbour?
5 Has Fumiko got long hair?
6 Have they got a dog?
7 Have I got your new mobile number?
8 Has he got a laptop?

3 1 a 2 b 3 a 4 a 5 b 6 b 7 a 8 b
4 Students' own answers.

47

1 a 1 hay 2 sore 3 temperature 4 stomach
5 back 6 cough 7 headache
8 toothache
b 1 e 2 a 3 h 4 g 5 b 6 f 7 d 8 c
2 a 1 are 2 well 3 matter 4 cold 5 dear
b 1 **A** Hello, Sandra. How are you?
B Oh, I'm not very well.
A Why? What's the matter?
B I've got a sore throat and a temperature.
A Oh, dear.
2 **A** Hello, Alan. How are you?
B Oh, I'm not very well.
A Why? What's the matter?
B I've got a bad back.
A Oh, dear.
3 1 smoke 2 exercise 3 salt 4 sun
5 vegetables

48

1 1 plasters 2 a piece of paper 3 a towel
4 scissors 5 a nail file 6 painkillers
7 a stamp 8 a pen 9 a mirror
10 tissues
2 a 1 some 2 any 3 any
b 1 a
2 some
3 any
4 a
5 any
6 some
3 1 got, Here, you
2 Have, any, haven't

Review: Lessons 45–48
1 b 2 a 3 b 4 a 5 b 6 a 7 a 8 a

49

1 ***go* + verb + *-ing***
swimming, skiing
***play* + sports**
football, golf
***play* + *the* + musical instruments**
the guitar, the piano
2 1 plays 2 go 3 play 4 goes 5 play
6 plays 7 go 8 go 9 play 10 go
3 1 go skating 2 plays golf 3 go dancing
4 plays the guitar 5 goes swimming
6 paints 7 sing 8 go skiing
4 Students' own answers.

50

1 1 He can't dance.
2 I can play the violin.
3 They can't sing.
4 He can play ice hockey.
5 She can't cook.
6 I can't swim.
2 1 Can he dance? No, he can't.
2 Can you play the violin? Yes, I can.
3 Can they sing? No, they can't.
4 Can he play ice hockey? Yes, he can.
5 Can she cook? No, she can't.
6 Can you swim? No, I can't.
3 a 1 h 2 g 3 f 4 a 5 b 6 d 7 e 8 c
b Students' own answers.
4 Students' own answers.

51

1 1 Yes, I can. 2 Japanese 3 No, I can't.
4 Yes, I can. 5 play volleyball and tennis
6 Yes, I can. 7 Yes, I can. 8 Yes, I can.
9 play the piano and the guitar
10 No, I can't. 11 Yes, I can.
2 Students' own answers.
3 Students' own answers.
4 Students' own answers.

52

1 1 F 2 F 3 T 4 T 5 F 6 F
2 1 e 2 d 3 a 4 b 5 c
3 a 1 Can I take 2 would be nice
3 Is Tuesday OK 4 I can't come
5 what about
b **A** Can I take you out to dinner?
B Yes, that would be nice.
A Is Friday OK for you?
B No, sorry. I can't come on Friday.
A Well, what about Saturday?
B Yes, Saturday's fine.

Review: Lessons 49–52
1 b 2 a 3 b 4 a 5 b 6 b 7 a 8 b

53

1 1 a bedroom 2 a window 3 the balcony
4 the garage 5 the garden 6 the kitchen
7 the hall 8 the stairs 9 the cellar
10 the dining room 11 the living room
12 downstairs 13 upstairs
14 the bathroom 15 a door
2 1 the dining room 4 a bedroom
2 the kitchen 5 the bathroom
3 the living room 6 the cellar
3 Students' own answers.

54

1 1 There's 2 There are 3 There's
4 There isn't 5 There aren't 6 There are
7 There isn't 8 There aren't
2 1 a 2 b 3 b 4 b 5 a 6 b
3 1 Is there 2 there is 3 are there
4 There are 5 Are there 6 there are
7 There's 8 Are there 9 there aren't
10 There's 11 Is there 12 there isn't
4 Students' own answers.

55

1 1 Scott 2 No 3 Yes
2 1 a modern 2 sports centre 3 four
4 living room 5 an office 6 bathrooms
7 ten 8 top 9 There's 10 on the balcony
3 Students' own answers.
4

Voiced *th* sound /θ/	**Unvoiced *th* sound /ð/**
bathroom	there
Thursday	these
thing	with
thirteen	mother
thanks	that

56

1 0 ground 1st first 2nd second 3rd third
4th fourth 5th fifth 6th sixth 7th seventh
8th eighth 9th ninth 10th tenth
11th eleventh 12th twelfth 13th thirteenth
14th fourteenth 15th fifteenth
2 1 29 2 31 3 32 4 27 5 28 6 30
3 1 can, fourth 2 there, on, street
3 is, over, door

Review: Lessons 53–56
1 b 2 a 3 b 4 a 5 b 6 a 7 b 8 b

57

1 1 socks 2 a suit 3 a shirt 4 trousers
5 a tie 6 a T-shirt 7 trainers 8 shorts
9 boots 10 a top 11 a jacket 12 shoes
13 a dress 14 jeans 15 a skirt
16 a jumper
2 **Singular**
jumper, jacket, T-shirt, dress
Plural
clothes, shorts, shoes, jeans
3 a 1 these, are they, They're
2 this, is it, It's
3 these, are they, They're
4 this, is it, It's
b **A** Do you like this jumper?
B Yes, I do. How much is it?
A It's £50.
A Do you like these shorts?
B Yes, I do. How much are they?
A They're €35.
4 Students' own answers.

58

1 1 She's 2 I'm 3 We're 4 They're
5 He's 6 You're 7 Lucy's 8 I'm
2 **+ *-ing***
go going play playing eat eating
reading, cleaning, sending
wear wearing
Remove *-e* + *-ing*
riding, having, writing
making, driving
Double consonant + *-ing*
running, sitting, getting
swim swimming
3 1 He's driving a sports car.
2 They're running.
3 She's taking a photograph.
4 We're watching TV.
5 He's getting up.
6 They're playing tennis.
4 1 I'm not reading a newspaper.
2 We aren't going to the supermarket.
3 They aren't playing golf.
4 He isn't wearing trainers.
5 She isn't having a shower.
6 I'm not using the computer.
7 You aren't eating my sandwich.
8 It isn't raining.
5 1 I'm wearing jeans.
I'm not wearing jeans.
2 I'm driving a car.
I'm not driving a car.
3 I'm sitting at a desk.
I'm not sitting at a desk.
4 I'm writing.
I'm not writing.
5 I'm swimming.
I'm not swimming.
6 I'm listening to music.
I'm not listening to music.
7 I'm watching TV.
I'm not watching TV.
8 I'm playing tennis.
I'm not playing tennis.

59

1 1 Meena 2 Sanjit 3 Michael 4 Tricia
5 Juanita 6 Elke

2 a 1 F 2 F 3 F 4 F 5 T 6 F 7 T 8 F
b 1 Tricia isn't drinking a cup of coffee.
2 Juanita and Elke aren't standing up.
3 Michael isn't sitting with Meena.
4 Tricia isn't talking to Elke.
6 Elke isn't reading a book.
8 Meena and Sanjit aren't eating.

3 1 flowers 2 a bottle of wine
3 a box of chocolates

60

1 Ryan gives Jordan a ticket for the football match. Jordan rings Lucy, but she is talking on her phone (*she isn't answering her phone*). Ryan leaves the coffee shop. Cindy is unhappy because her sister (*her parents*) is coming. Lucy is leaving her flat (*her office*). Her friends are going to the cinema, (*a rock concert*) but she isn't going with them. She is going on a date with Ryan (*Jordan*). At nine (*eight*) o'clock, Lucy is sitting alone at home (*in the restaurant*). Ryan and Jordan are watching a rock concert (*football match*). Peter sees them on TV.

2 1 See you tomorrow. 3 See you later.
2 Have a nice time. 4 I won't be long.

3 1 See you later. 2 Have a nice time.
I won't be long. See you tomorrow.

Review: Lessons 57–60
1 a 2 b 3 b 4 a 5 a 6 a 7 b 8 b

61

1

T	R	A	[1]M			
		C	[2]O	A	C	H
			[3]T	A	X	I
		B	[4]O	A	T	
	C	A	[5]R			
			[6]B	U	S	
T	R	A	[7]I	N		
	B	I	[8]K	E		
		F	[9]E	R	R	Y

2 1 a bus stop 2 the underground 3 a station
4 an airport 5 a bus station 6 a taxi rank

3 1 c 2 e 3 d 4 a 5 b

4 1 b 2 b 3 a 4 b 5 a 6 a 7 b

5 1 travel station 5 late flat
2 plane train ✓ 6 bank make
3 taxi bag ✓ 7 place have
4 take wait ✓ 8 play table ✓

62

1 1 Are they waiting for the bus?
2 Is she having lunch?
3 Are you having a good time?
4 Am I sitting in your seat?
5 Are we taking the underground?
6 Are you watching the news?
7 Is the computer working now?
8 Are the trains running late?

2 1 b 2 d 3 f 4 g 5 e 6 a 7 c

3 1 What are you eating?
2 Where are they going?
3 What is she wearing?
4 What are they doing?
5 Who are you waiting for?
6 What are you watching?

4 1 a 2 b 3 b 4 a 5 b 6 b

5 Students' own answers.

63

1 1 on 2 in 3 in 4 on 5 on 6 on
7 on 8 in 9 in 10 on

2 a A 2 B 1
b 1 1 sitting 2 swimming 3 looking after
4 writing 5 having

2 1 travelling 2 taking 3 doing 4 enjoying

3 1 a 2 b 3 b 4 a 5 b 6 a

4 Students' own answers.

64

1 1 he's going to the dentist's
2 he's meeting visitors
3 he's taking the visitors to the airport
4 he's playing basketball
5 he's going to Bruno's party
6 he's looking after the children
7 he's having lunch with Elena's parents

2 Students' own answers.

3 1 c 2 e 3 a 4 b 5 d

Review: Lessons 61–64
1 b 2 b 3 a 4 a 5 a 6 b 7 b 8 b

65

1 **in:** a meeting, bed, the garden, the shower
at: home, a party, the doctor's, work, the supermarket, a restaurant

2 1 in a meeting 2 in bed 3 in the shower
4 at a restaurant 5 at school
6 in the garden 7 at the supermarket
8 at work

3 1 on holiday 2 here 3 in 4 out 5 away

4 Students' own answers.

66

1 1 1 were 2 was 3 was 4 were 5 were
2 1 was 2 was 3 were
3 1 was 2 was 3 were 4 were

2 1 I wasn't 2 They weren't 3 He wasn't
4 We weren't 5 Ela wasn't 6 You weren't

3 **the past**
last week, yesterday, yesterday evening
the present
today, tonight

4 1 I wasn't in last night.
I was at the sports centre.
2 She was ill yesterday.
She wasn't at work.
3 I was in the shower.
I wasn't in bed.
4 We weren't at home last night.
We were at the cinema.
5 The hotel was very good.
It wasn't expensive.

5 Students' own answers.

6 **one syllable**
don't, weren't, aren't, can't
two syllables
isn't, wasn't, doesn't, haven't, hasn't

67

1 1 Were you out yesterday afternoon?
2 Were they on holiday last week?
3 Was Mohammed at a football match on Friday?
4 Was the film good?
5 Was Sunita at the dentist's on Tuesday morning?
6 Were we at the supermarket last Wednesday?
7 Was he late on Monday?
8 Were you at the meeting?

2 a and b
1 **A** Were Mick and Rosie away last week?
B Yes, they were.
2 **A** Were they on holiday?
B Yes, they were.
3 **A** Were they in Turkey?
B No, they weren't.
4 **A** Was Rosie ill?
B Yes, she was.
5 **A** Was she in bed for two days?
B No, she wasn't.

3 Students' own answers.

4 1 the USA 2 the UK 3 the UK
4 the USA 5 the USA

68

1 1 c 2 a 3 g 4 d 5 f 6 b 7 e

2 a 1 I'm very angry with you. 2 That's it!
3 Don't talk to me!
4 It was very embarrassing.
b b Lucy

3 1 was 2 was 3 weren't 4 were 5 wasn't
6 was 7 were 8 wasn't 9 was 10 were

Review: Lessons 65–68
1 a 2 a 3 b 4 b 5 b 6 b 7 a 8 b

69

1 **Medical services** a paramedic, an ambulance, a hospital, a first aid kit
The fire brigade a fire fighter, a fire engine, a fire station, a fire alarm
The police a police officer, a police car, a police station

2 1 c 2 d 3 a 4 b

3 a 1 F 2 F 3 T 4 F 5 T 6 F
b Students' own answers.

70

1 a 1 decided 2 finished 3 called
4 sounded 5 picked 6 rushed
b 1 arrived 2 closed 3 waited
4 started 5 opened 6 travelled
c 1 arrived 2 stayed 3 watched
4 rained 5 travelled 6 needed

2 Students' own answers.

3 a and b

	Present simple	**Past simple**	**Extra syllable?**
1	stop (1)	stopped (1)	
2	start (1)	started (2)	✓
3	watch (1)	watched (1)	
4	use (1)	used (1)	
5	need (1)	needed (2)	✓
6	wait (1)	waited (2)	✓
7	arrive (2)	arrived (2)	
8	decide (2)	decided (3)	✓
9	walk (1)	walked (1)	
10	want (1)	wanted (2)	✓

71

1 a 1 c 2 d
b 1 Jill's friend 2 Jill's husband 3 Jill's son

2 1 F 2 T 3 T 4 F 5 T 6 F 7 F 8 T 9 F 10 F

3 1 Faith invited Jill to lunch because it was Jill's birthday.
2 Faith and Jill were friends because they were at school together.
3 Jill called the police because there were voices in the living room.
4 The police officers laughed because there wasn't a burglar in the room.
5 Peter came home because it was his mum's birthday.
6 There were voices in the living room because the TV was on.

72

1 January February March April May June July August September October November December

2 1 twenty-fourth 2 second 3 sixteenth 4 twenty-eighth 5 thirty-first 6 ninth 7 twentieth 8 tenth 9 thirtieth 10 twenty-third

3 1 the first of October
2 the seventh of April
3 the fourteenth of May
4 the thirtieth of September
5 the twenty-first of February
6 the third of November
7 the twenty-second of August
8 the nineteenth of March
9 the twelfth of July
10 the twentieth of December

Review: Lessons 69–72
1 b 2 a 3 a 4 a 5 b 6 a 7 b 8 b

73

1 1 I 2 R 3 R 4 I 5 I 6 I 7 R 8 I 9 R 10 I 11 R 12 I 13 I 14 R 15 R 16 I

2

A	L	E	F	T	W	Z	G	N	W	X	W
P	B	E	A	W	M	B	O	B	O	Q	R
R	C	N	H	A	D	T	T	F	A	F	O
D	R	A	N	K	U	C	V	Z	D	V	T
K	L	Q	S	L	B	O	U	G	H	T	E
W	J	M	D	C	Y	E	C	X	K	E	R
E	M	A	P	I	J	E	D	O	V	R	K
N	R	D	E	F	D	J	A	O	A	L	T
T	D	E	Y	C	T	U	R	B	T	Z	O
I	G	S	D	G	X	D	I	H	E	G	O
B	C	A	M	E	I	S	A	W	N	Y	K
T	H	U	H	O	F	O	U	N	D	V	M

3 1 arrived
2 bought
3 did
4 drove
5 got
6 had
7 helped
8 made
9 needed
10 phoned
11 played
12 saw
13 started
14 took
15 travelled
16 waited

4 1 got up 2 went 3 met 4 decided 5 saw 6 invited 7 came 8 put 9 drove 10 arrived 11 got 12 ate 13 sat 14 played 15 swam 16 was 17 left 18 had

5 Students' own answers.

74

1 1 didn't wake up
2 didn't take
3 didn't finish
4 didn't send
5 didn't like
6 didn't rain
7 didn't go
8 didn't buy

2 1 We didn't play football. We played basketball.
2 They went skating. They didn't go skiing.
3 He didn't take the bus. He took a taxi.
4 She bought some clothes. She didn't buy a TV.

3 1 b 2 a 3 b 4 a 5 a 6 b

4 Students' own answers.

5 1 They went to the cinema.
2 I didn't have lunch.
3 We bought a new car.
4 He didn't play tennis.
5 She got up late.
6 We stayed at home.

75

1 a 1 Teresa 2 Callum 3 Mona 4 Lucas
b 1 Buenos Aires 2 Bilbao 3 Madrid 4 Sydney

2 1 f 2 e 3 a 4 g 5 b 6 h 7 d 8 c

3 Students' own answers.

4 Students' own answers.

76

1 1 Lucy was right. 2 It was Ryan's fault. 3 It wasn't my fault.

2 1 my, John's 2 his, her 3 Kirsty's, Tim's 4 our, their 5 girl's, boy's

3 1 left 2 saw 3 told 4 wasn't 5 was 6 went 7 tried 8 sent 9 didn't know 10 wanted 11 didn't go 12 had 13 went

Review: Lessons 73–76
1 b 2 a 3 b 4 a 5 a 6 b 7 b 8 a

77

1 1 d 2 f 3 e 4 a 5 g 6 h 7 c 8 b

2 1 Tom went to the park.
2 Ana did the washing.
3 Adrien tidied the living room.
4 I paid the bills.
5 Sam washed the car.
6 Victor visited his family.
7 David worked in the garden.
8 We met our friends.

3 1 parents 2 theatre 3 shopping 4 garden 5 cinema 6 park 7 friends 8 house

4 Students' own answers.

78

1 1 1 Did you have 2 had 3 didn't have 4 had
2 1 went 2 did you go 3 didn't go 4 went
3 1 Did you make 2 made 3 didn't make 4 made

2 1 I did, she didn't 2 they didn't, they did 3 we didn't, we did 4 he did, we did

3 1 Did Kelly visit 2 Did you clean 3 Did we leave 4 Did Bill find 5 Did it rain

4 a 1 Did you have 2 Did you buy 3 Did you go 4 Did you do 5 Did you meet 6 Did you watch
b Students' own answers.

79

1 1 have 2 do 3 went 4 paid 5 met 6 go 7 went 8 watched 9 have 10 wanted 11 went 12 buy 13 bought 14 looked 15 didn't buy 16 do 17 didn't do 18 tidied 19 relaxed 20 visited

2 1 Where did you go?
2 What time did they arrive?
3 How did you travel?
4 Who did she meet?
5 When did the concert finish?
6 What did you buy?
7 Why did he leave?
8 Where did you have lunch?

3 a 1 What time did you get up today?
2 What did you have for breakfast?
3 What did you watch on TV last night?
4 What did you do last Saturday morning?
5 What did you do last Sunday?
6 Where did you go on your last holiday?
7 What time did you go to bed last night?
8 How did you travel to work / school?
b Students' own answers.

80

1 ***at* + times** six thirty, night
***in* + parts of the day** the afternoon, the evening
***on* + • days • parts of specific days • dates** 12th March, Monday afternoon

2 1 f 2 e 3 d 4 b 5 a 6 c

3 1 did you do 2 went 3 did you see 4 saw 5 Was 6 it wasn't, were, didn't like

4 **A** What did you do on Saturday?
B We went to the beach.
A Who did you go with?
B I went with my family.
A Was the weather good?
B Yes, it was.

Review: Lessons 77–80
1 b 2 a 3 b 4 a 5 b 6 b 7 a 8 a